Mary Ann,

May **THE GRACIOUS MYSTERY**

continue to bless you.

Jim Bacik

THE GRACIOUS MYSTERY

Finding God in Ordinary Experience

James J. Bacik

Nihil Obstat: Rev. Lawrence Landini, O.F.M.
Rev. John J. Jennings

Imprimi Potest: Rev. Jeremy Harrington, O.F.M.
Provincial

Imprimatur: + James H. Garland, V.G.
Archdiocese of Cincinnati
November 4, 1986

The nihil obstat and *imprimatur* are a declaration that a book or pamphlet is considered to be free from doctrinal or moral error. It is not implied that those who have granted the *nihil obstat* and *imprimatur* agree with the contents, opinions or statements expressed.

Scripture texts used in this work are taken from the *New American Bible*, copyright ©1970 by the Confraternity of Christian Doctrine, Washington, D.C., and are used by permission of the copyright owner. All rights reserved.

The following essays were previously published in modified form in the *National Catholic Reporter:* "Dealing With Fundamentalists," "The Faces of Evil: Learning From Fiction Writers," "Dealing With Tragedy: The Challenger Disaster," "Martin Luther King: Drum Major for Justice," "Christian Commitment: Church and World," and "A Contemporary Creed."

Book design by Robert Roose

Cover by Barron Krody

SBN 0-86716-072-1

For my mother,
Lillian Marie Bacik,
loving heart of the family,
wise teacher of self-acceptance,
faithful witness of the Gracious Mystery.

Contents

Introduction
Alert to Mystery

In my work as a campus minister, I speak with many people who want to discuss serious matters: A grad student in philosophy expresses a desire for an attractive contemporary model of the good and virtuous life. A young woman victimized by repressive sexual training wants to learn how to relate better with her boyfriend. A recent graduate disappointed with the corrupt practices of the business world is searching for a more fulfilling career. A shy fellow wants to learn how to be more comfortable with people. A vibrant woman, often distracted as she flits from one new experience to another, wants to learn how to focus her attention on what is at hand. Four business majors tired of accounting classes are looking for a book about important life issues to read and discuss. An activist professor, pulled by the many demands on his time, searches for roots to sustain him. An angry, hurt husband seeks healing so that he can restore his relationship with his wife.

These individuals are typical of a growing number of people involved in what might be termed a religious or spiritual search—even though they may not call it that. For them it is not simply a matter of improving their prayer life, or discovering the Bible, or learning a meditation technique, or finding a more vibrant liturgy—although all of this may be involved. Their spiritual pursuit is focused on a quest for meaning in the midst of absurdity, for commitment in the face of multiple options, for a deeper life amidst the temptation to superficiality. It is a search

1

Introduction

for an ultimate concern which overcomes the dullness of life, for a wholeness which pulls together a fragmented existence, for an overarching framework which provides a context for daily concerns. For many today the emphasis is not on the other world, but this one; not on sin or guilt, but personal growth; not on limiting the human, but discovering a richer way of living humanly.

The Eclipse of Mystery

Our dominant culture, unfortunately, offers few resources for responding to these deeper longings of the human heart. We live in a world suffering from an eclipse of mystery.

Mystery is that which eludes rational control, which defies logical calculation and which exceeds all imagining. Mystery is that which sustains and draws us while remaining forever inexhaustible. When mystery is perceived as friendly, we commonly name it God.

For many today this Gracious Mystery is hidden, forgotten, distorted or encased in a zone of silence. Life becomes a problem to be solved rather than a mystery to be contemplated.

In such a culture it is difficult to find a language for discussing the most significant matters. Sin is reduced to neurosis, sex becomes a matter of performance, death is ignored or disguised, time is money, the future is predictable. The "cult of the computer" tempts people to view science as a religion, to expect technology to solve all our human problems, to trust data more than personal insight, to abdicate responsibility to experts, even to begin to think of themselves and others as nothing more than sophisticated machines.

Such a one-dimensional world generates its own discontents. Persons tend to feel suffocated, subject to the blahs, strangely apathetic, tired of the rat race, at loose ends, without roots, excessively anxious. In this situation there is a natural tendency to grasp for security by looking for simple answers and to reject complexity by breaking out of the ordinary. We find examples of this in the interest in the occult, the fascination with astrology, the appeal of soap operas, the desire for simplistic political and economic solutions, and the rise of religious fundamentalism. We also see a growing number of people in our culture who report striking conversion experiences, prize spectacular gifts such as speaking in tongues and claim unmistakable messages from God.

This "cult of the spectacular" offers itself as an escape from the "cult of the computer." But it has its own dangers. In this "cult of the spectacular," only those with striking religious experiences walk in the light. Those with a more pedestrian piety are relegated to the darkness.

It is not unusual for me to encounter solid Catholic parents who are terribly hurt because their "born-again" son or daughter has accused them of not being genuine Christians. Unfortunately, these exclusivist tendencies manifested by some "pipeline believers," who speak as though they have direct, unambiguous communications with God, often obscure the positive aspects of the contemporary evangelical and charismatic renewal.

Many of the people I talk to are both dissatisfied with the superficiality of the "cult of the computer" and leery of the excesses of the "cult of the spectacular." We need another alternative. It is the purpose of these essays to explore what this alternative spirituality would look like, what some of its characteristics might be and how it could help us reflect on various aspects of our contemporary experience.

A More Human Way

The spirituality for which people today yearn must be several things: First, it must be *contemporary* in that it draws on the best insights of modern theology. Second, it must be *dialectical*, that is, responsive to the paradoxical complexity of human life. Third, it must be *American*, that is, rooted in our indigenous experience as citizens of the United States.

Contemporary theology does provide a framework for building an alternative spirituality. In brief outline form, here is what it says:

> We humans, in all our longings and struggles, are supported and drawn by a Gracious Mystery which we call God. This Holy Mystery, willing wholeness and final fulfillment for all of us, offers every human being a share in the divine life.

This grace creates in us an inner word, a call of conscience, an impulse to the good.

When we respond positively to this universal revelation, we act as people of faith and move closer to our God. All our experiences can mediate this presence of the Gracious Mystery.

We live and move in a grace-filled world where all things are potentially revelatory, where there are signals of hope in our ordinary experiences, where there are surprising resources in our own hearts. In fact, our genuine experience of self is precisely our experience of God. Thus our task is to be on alert so as to find the light in the darkness, the Infinite in our finite experience.

For us Christians, Jesus Christ is the never-to-be-surpassed high point of the divine/human encounter. His story illumines and directs our lives by shaping our consciousness according to his values, by attuning us to the presence of the Father, by assuring us that our efforts are ultimately worthwhile. Putting on the mind of Christ means that we actually experience life in a renewed way, perceiving depths previously eclipsed and hearing demands formerly ignored.

In a previous book, *Apologetics and the Eclipse of Mystery* (University of Notre Dame Press, 1980), I employed this type of theology drawn from the work of the great German Jesuit Karl Rahner (1904-1984) in order to construct models of mystery. These models, composed of a theological framework and descriptions of common human experiences, were designed to guide our quest to probe the mysterious depths of our lives. Now, in this book, I want to apply those ideas to specific problems and experiences which we face in the United States today. My purpose is to respond to the needs described above for a spirituality which is contemporary, American and dialectical.

Spirituality-in-the-Making

One way I have found to carry out my role as spiritual guide over the last few years is by writing short essays every couple of weeks for a group of people—some of whom gathered to discuss them. A selected number of these essays are collected here with the hope they can become a spur for personal reflection and group discussion to an even wider audience.

These essays obviously do not comprise a comprehensive contemporary spirituality. I hope the themes running throughout, however, will help push us in that direction: the need to stay in touch with concrete experience; the value of working out a solid understanding of human nature; the effort to find God in the ordinary things of life; the importance of dealing constructively with the inevitable tensions of life; the hope-filled conviction that, in and through the struggles of life, the Gracious One is to be found—the God who is revealed to us by Jesus of Nazareth.

The essays which follow are divided into two parts. Those in Part One set a framework for cultivating a deeper awareness of self and of God.

Chapter One essays describe the life of the Spirit and link our spiritual experience with biblical language about the Holy Spirit. This chapter also suggests ways our imagination can put us in touch with this world of the Spirit. Chapter Two suggests some of the attitudes needed as we pursue the spiritual quest: self-acceptance, a healthy trust of experience, a proper outlook on the future, and a solid theology of miracles.

Chapter Three recommends three dialectical virtues: committed openness, hopeful realism and reflective spontaneity. These are especially helpful in staying in touch with the mysterious depths of our experience. They are called *dialectical* virtues because they reflect the paradoxical nature of our quest for authentic selfhood in which we are always struggling to achieve a synthesis of apparently conflicting tendencies and demands.

Chapter Four examines some of the commonly experienced obstacles to spiritual development: our own sinfulness, the complexity and superficiality of modern culture, and the doubts sown by the exclusive claims of fundamentalists.

In the essays in Part Two of the book, I reflect on some concrete experiences of persons and events which have given me insight and inspiration. Chapter Five describes some encounters with the dark forces in life: compulsions; the many faces of evil; disasters, such as the Challenger tragedy; and death itself. And in Chapter Six, we encounter three great 20th-century

Introduction

figures—Dorothy Day, Thomas Merton, Martin Luther King—and try to discern their significance for our spiritual life.

Chapter Seven examines our ordinary life in the world of athletics, work and family for clues to the mysterious presence of the Spirit. In the eighth and final chapter, I reflect on the deeper meanings in our celebrations of feasts and seasons such as Ash Wednesday, Thanksgiving, Advent, Christmas and autumn. The Epilogue attempts to pull together many of the thoughts in the book by presenting a short creed or summary statement of the Christian faith.

The following essays are my attempt to use the kind of theological framework outlined above to discern the extraordinary in the midst of the ordinary, to isolate bits of human experience in order to probe their deeper meaning. Many people tell me there is a need for a level of spiritual writing which mediates between the academic approaches of the theological journals and a more popular audience. I hope these essays help respond to this need.

I invite the reader constantly to measure the experiences in these essays against his or her own experience. And I hope these essays can jog consciousness, open up new horizons and lead to personal insights in the search for the Mystery we call God.

Part One
A Framework for Exploring the Mystery

The eclipse of mystery is a stubborn problem in the contemporary world. Blindness and illusion remain a part of our common experience. We need both a receptive spirit and a systematic effort to attune ourselves to the mysterious source of our being. The attitudes, perspectives and advice discussed in this first part of the book can help us sharpen our perception of the Mystery which continues to support and allure us.

Chapter One
The Experience of Spirit

What Is 'Spirit'?

As we begin to explore the spiritual life it is crucial that we have a proper understanding of the word *spirit*. The way that we respond both intellectually and emotionally to this key notion provides clues to some of our fundamental attitudes toward life.

Many conceive spirit as "that which is opposed to matter." The prime model for this approach sees the soul as the spiritual principle placed in us to enliven the material body. We are a composite made up of two distinct realities fused together as we sojourn on this earth.

Within this general understanding of human nature, some people sense a great contrast and opposition between spirit and matter: Spirit is good and elevating, while matter is evil and debasing. The soul is imprisoned in the body and salvation comes when the soul breaks loose from this enslavement and goes up to heaven.

This outlook leads to a spirituality that fears involvement in the world. Such a spirituality sees physical pleasure as evil; considers the body as excess baggage on the journey to heaven; devalues human work and effort; insists on mortification and strict rules to control the unruly material principle; distrusts human emotions.

This understanding of "soul *vs.* body"—and the spirituality that flows from it—may seem foreign to many of us in all its aspects. Yet it is important to ask: *In what ways do we find traces of it in our own attitudes and behavior?*

9

A Framework

Is there *another way* of understanding the word *spirit*? How can we discover and ground a healthier notion of the spiritual dimension of our existence? Let us begin by examining our experience.

First of all, we know ourselves, for the most part, as a single entity in a concrete world of people and things. We are part of this world, involved in its activities and dependent on it as our environment.

But we are not completely caught up in this world. We have the power to distance ourselves from it, to stand back and make judgments about it, to withdraw into ourselves, to form ideas about our world. Rocks just sit there, and animals seem to respond instinctively; but we humans can gather ourselves and respond creatively to our world.

This unique ability supplies part of the experiential base for understanding the spiritual dimension of our existence: *We are "spirit" to the degree that we can accomplish this distancing, gathering and centering of ourselves.*

Second, as we reflect on our existence as a unified person in a world of relationships, we find that no particular thing or person seems to satisfy us totally. There is a dynamism inside us that overflows everything we encounter.

We possess longings that seem to aim at the infinite. Our hearts are indeed restless. Persons, possessions, achievement, success, status, pleasure may temporarily arrest the drives and may even lull us into a false sense of tranquility. But the infinite longings have a way of reasserting themselves as they transcend every earthly resting place.

Here again we find an experiential base for understanding our spiritual dimension: *We know ourselves to be "spirit" insofar as we transcend every particular person or thing in a drive toward an infinite goal.*

We can explore our understanding of *matter* in much the same way. While it seems simpler and easier to touch a face or kick a chair, we will derive a more useful understanding by reflecting again on our self-experience.

One of the first ways we know ourselves as material beings is in our experience of *limitation*. It is true that we can distance ourselves from our world, but we can't do it completely. We can stand back to make judgments, but our world has a way of maintaining a hold on us and clouding our judgments. We can center ourselves and form ideas about our environment, but we can never gain the perspective needed to understand the whole of it. In short, we experience ourselves as limited, as a finite spirit.

It is the material dimension of our existence which accounts for this limitation. We are "bodied" creatures, with physical senses that cannot be totally self-possessed.

Such limitations are again evident as we consider our infinite longings. While we strive for a distant, mysterious goal, we never attain it. Although we desire a final resting place, it is denied to us. If we were pure spirits the daily drudgery of walking gradually toward the desired goal would be avoided. As it is, we know ourselves as bodily creatures subject to the laws of time and space, as finite spirits limited by a material principle.

Our *anthropology* (that is, our understanding of human nature) largely determines our *spirituality*. If we begin, therefore, by understanding ourselves as composed of two distinct elements (body and soul) stuck together in a temporary union, we will always be in danger of denying one or the other. We will be tempted toward either a world-denying spiritualism or a flat, self-contained materialism.

If we begin, on the other hand, with our experience of ourselves as single, unified persons with *infinite* longings and *finite* capabilities, we are in a position to understand "spirit" in a very different—integrated—way. "Spirit," then, points to the vital, exciting part of our experience. Spirit involves the essential business of centering and integrating, the distinctively human power of understanding and judging. Spirit means the ability to transcend the present facts and to dream of a better future. We are spirited bodies, restless hearts capable of moving gradually toward a fulfilling future.

From this perspective spirit cannot be dismissed as an unproven, mysterious addition to the very real material world. Nor can discussion of the spiritual life be dismissed as a mere theoretical exercise, divorced from the real concerns of contemporary people. Rather, *"spirit" and "spirituality" are revealed to be at the center of human existence and any reflection on it.*

Experiencing the Holy Spirit

A general discussion of "spirit" raises questions about our Christian understanding of the Holy Spirit. For example: Today we commonly speak about the Holy Spirit empowering people to work for human liberation. What does this mean? Let me begin by recalling a concrete example from my own experience:

Anger is too mild a word. She is in a *rage* over the situation of women in the Church. As a member of a religious order she has given many years of service to the Christian community and she now feels frustrated and betrayed. Some people in Rome who are out of touch with the situation in the United States are trying to tell her community how to dress and how to organize themselves. The case of Agnes Mansour still sticks in her mind. Where is due process, simple justice, respect for a good and talented woman?

The rage colors everything. She views the unsuspecting priest who comes to celebrate Mass in the midst of a community meeting as an intruder. Sisters who are too comfortable with the status quo become linked, in her mind, with the enemy.

Does this mean she is going to leave the community and repudiate the Church? An emphatic no! Surprisingly she feels, even in the midst of the pain and frustration, a renewed sense of solidarity with her religious order and, in a mysterious way, with the Church as a whole.

As I listen to this poignant tale, an immediate empathy for this woman rises from within. I feel myself drawn out of the constricting area where my self-centered concerns dominate. An initial bonding is established. The rage is uniquely hers, yet I really think I know something of what she is feeling. This motivates me to increase my efforts to see and feel the whole problem from her viewpoint.

This reaching out in empathy succeeds in part and then propels me to look within myself where an objective analysis begins forming. This alternating process of reaching out in empathy and of returning to self will not only enable me to be an effective helper for this woman, it will also provide the basis for knowing myself as spirit and understanding religious language about the Holy Spirit.

Our personal relationships do indeed provide a fruitful basis for analyzing the spiritual dimension of our being. We can communicate with one another because we have the ability to abstract universal concepts from individual things. Human beings fall in love because they are able to break out of the prison of selfishness and reach out to another with care and passion. Some of our most significant learning occurs when we pass over to the viewpoint of others and then return to our own standpoint modified and enriched.

There is a twofold movement in our personal relationships. In the first we go outside ourselves, reach out, move beyond our supposed limits, transcend material boundaries and establish common ground with other unique individuals. In the second, we return to self, draw inward, distance ourselves from others, think our own thoughts and dwell in an inner space where we know our own uniqueness. In both movements we experience ourselves as individuals who transcend the material and who defy rational calculation and empirical analysis.

In short, we are spirit because we can love and learn and communicate. The spiritual dimension of my own being becomes evident in my ability both to empathize and advise my Sister friend as she struggles with her rage.

But there is more to it. These root abilities are often experienced as a *gift* beyond our own making and a *call* beyond our own choosing. They are encompassed by mystery.

The impulse to transcend our selfishness and establish solidarity with others comes unbidden. Surprises are in store when we enter into honest interaction with others. Empathy for a few individuals serves as a reminder of a hidden unity with all people. Trying to help another person can bring a mysterious inner peace. The right word of counsel comes to our lips and we wonder where it came from. Hope remains in our hearts even when there appears to be no way to help a friend. An absorbing conversation brings to light unexpected insights. *It is in conjunction with such experiences of a mysterious gift and call that talk of the Holy Spirit makes most sense.*

Biblical language about the Spirit illuminates the deeper meaning of our experience and encourages us to be responsive to our better impulses. The Holy Spirit is, for example, the one who draws us into communion with the Father and the Son and gives us a sense of solidarity with all human beings (1 Cor 12). The Spirit gives us hope in abundance (Rom 15:13) and strengthens us inwardly (Eph 3:16). It is the work of the Spirit to reveal the deeper secrets and purposes of life and to get us in touch with our unique gifts (1 Cor 2:10-13). The courage to be bold in speaking the truth (Acts 4:31) and resourceful in reaching out to others (Acts 10:44-48) is due to the power of the Spirit.

In John's Gospel the teaching on the Spirit reaches its culmination. Here we read about another Paraclete who is sent by Jesus to be an intercessor and a personal presence in the ongoing life of the community. This Counselor will teach the truth and challenge the evil in the world (Jn 14—16).

There is another aspect of the Spirit, however, revealed by my friend's rage over women's situation in the Church. We are dealing here with newly perceived *injustice*. Gifts of the Spirit meant for building up the Body of Christ are being denied or neglected. The power of the Church to be an authentic sign of human dignity and solidarity is diminished. It is one more example of a world where social sin is a reality.

Systems can be unjust and can stifle the human spirit. All institutions are in danger of neglecting the individual and of oppressing particular groups. Even the Church, with its tremendous potential for liberating people, can end up constricting some of its members.

Again the scriptural notion of the Spirit helps us to interpret this situation. Luke gives us the image of Jesus the liberator who says,

> The spirit of the Lord is upon me;
> therefore he has anointed me.
> He has sent me to bring glad tidings to the poor,
> to proclaim liberty to captives,
> Recovery of sight to the blind
> and release to prisoners,... (Lk 4:18)

When we deny our constructive impulses and give in to

behavior which brings division and strife into the community, Scripture suggests that we grieve the Spirit of God (Eph 4:25-32). The real call is to be responsive to the Spirit whose fruit is "love, joy, peace, patient endurance, kindness, generosity, faith, mildness and chastity" (Gal 5:22-23).

Rage over injustice is understandable. The Spirit calls us to transform it into constructive action. We can see the work of the Spirit among those who join together with others of like mind to help feed the hungry, free political prisoners, find shelter for the homeless and jobs for the unemployed. The Holy Spirit gives energy for the long haul even when little progress is made.

Where intelligence is used to fight systemic evil, we believe the Spirit of truth is active. Talk of the Spirit empowering people to work for human liberation makes sense when we see individuals and groups struggling for justice with great courage or quiet constancy.

Finally, we must remember that we cannot imprison the Holy Spirit in our small minds and limited categories. When the Sister surprised me with her comment about remaining in solidarity with the community despite her anger, I understood in a deeper way that the Spirit is the One who always exceeds our expectations and breaks through our conventional ways of thinking.

Imagination: A Channel of the Spirit

Our ability to imagine is a great resource in cultivating a deeper appreciation of the Spirit which surrounds us. Through our imagination we are able to drift back into our social and personal history, to relive important moments, to reexperience previous joys and sorrows. The *past* can be brought into the present and shaped according to our current needs and interests. We can bask in last summer's sun in the midst of a blizzard, or stand up to the bully who once intimidated us.

The spiritual power of imagining can also propel us into the *future* as we dream dreams, envision possibilities, set goals and make plans. Our daydreams can envision moments of great triumph as well as dismal failure, scenes which produce exhilaration as well as anxiety. Our hearts can soar in anticipation of meeting an old friend and our palms can sweat before we ever get to the dentist's chair.

Imagination also functions in the *present* as we interpret our world, find creative solutions to problems, create works of art, impose meaning on the buzzing confusion around us, tell stories and form our self-image. We can interpret the smile of a friend as a gift because we imagine ourselves immersed in a world of spirit which is gracious.

Imagination enables us to reconstruct our past and project ourselves into the future while immersing ourselves in the present moment.

Imagination is also linked with the kind of daydreaming and fantasy which breaks down the usual social conventions, goes beyond our logical assessment of what is possible, and overwhelms our rational perceptions of what is real. Therefore, one can imagine: talking to a deceased loved one; seducing a beautiful woman; freeing all political prisoners; building a model city of justice and harmony.

Such daydreaming is often dismissed, however, as an idle waste of time. Or our fantasies are judged too embarrassing to admit to ourselves, let alone anyone else. The importance of the imagination has been eclipsed by the Enlightenment idea of a rational, logical approach to reality. Hardheaded realists do not talk of what *could* be, but of what *is*.

Given this cultural bias we need, by way of corrective, to listen to those who give imagination a more central place in an analysis of what it means to be human. A good place to begin is with 20th-century Marxist philosopher Ernst Bloch. His analysis of daydreams and human hope has influenced our contemporary Christian theology of hope.

For Bloch, human beings are essentially constituted by their ability to dream of a better future and to strive to achieve it. We walk a narrow line between a "now" which is always incomplete and disappearing and a "not yet" which is ever newly appearing.

Despite his atheism, Bloch has a positive view of Jesus. He sees Jesus as one who brought into the world the consciousness of the beginning of a new age, thus enabling us to see ourselves as people who must hope for a better future.

Bloch's favorite mythological figure is Prometheus who, by stealing fire from the gods, becomes not only a rebel but the patron of human adventurousness. For Bloch the true "original sin" is not the pride of wanting to be like God. It is rather that loss of nerve which leads us to abandon our desire to be like God.

Since the best is still pending, and must be trusted to succeed, we must dream grand visions. Small wishes bore us and are forgotten, but great dreams endure and are carried all the way to the grave.

Bloch suggests that our daydreams are even more valuable than night dreams in achieving a deeper self-understanding. Our deepest wishes are revealed in our daydreams in an unguarded and daring manner. In general, our daydreams reveal the unfinished character of our lives: that we do not have a fixed essence but are in process of creating ourselves; that we have a responsibility to guide our existence into a better future.

Our fantasy life also manifests the distorted character of human existence: the contradictions present in our hearts, the fact that we are moved by tendencies which are opposed to our stated ideals, the disparity between a world filled with injustice and hatred and our dream of a universal community of love.

In summary, then, *our daydreams open up the spiritual world by reminding us of the possibilities of human existence*, the unrealized potential which is locked up in the core of our being, the truth hidden beneath the ordinariness of life, the overlooked goodness in other people, and the hope for a better world.

But some cautions are in order. Imagination, just as much as reason, is an ambivalent faculty. It can distort the spiritual search and lead astray as well as reveal and constructively transform.

No doubt some people spend too much time daydreaming. The married man struggling to remain faithful to his wife may find he has to keep careful control over his fantasies about other women. For some, the world of fantasy overwhelms reality, thus impairing effectiveness in the everyday world. Fantasy can become an escape from the hard and risky business of creating healthy personal relationships. Nostalgia, as an attempt to return to a past which was safe and more comfortable, can blunt our desire to help transform our dangerous and uncomfortable world. Concentration on dreaming of a better future can cause people to miss the current opportunities for enjoyment and enrichment. In short, a romantic, uncritical acceptance of a free-flowing, unprincipled imagination is as destructive of our efforts to be authentically human as a one-dimensional rationalism.

On the other hand, imagination can be a valuable corrective to an overly rational and manipulative approach to reality. By developing and sensitizing our imaginations through reading fiction and poetry, immersing ourselves in nature and meditating regularly, we will learn to appreciate the mysterious depth of our world. Attention to our daydreams, which reveal our hidden desires and interests, provides helpful clues in our quest for authentic growth. If we sense the gap between the image of an ideal community of universal love and the actual alienation in our world, we are more likely to engage in constructive action on behalf of social justice. By imagining a better future for ourselves and staying alert to the signals of hope in our world, we can help avoid the paralysis of depression and the meaninglessness of routine activity. Regular imaginative recall of happy past experiences and personal triumphs can help in overcoming a despondent disposition and poor self-image. A bit of escapist fantasizing can help renew our spirit and energize us for the current tasks. In brief, the cultivation of our imagination is a vital element in our growth toward a richer spiritual life and fuller human existence.

Our imagination also has an explicitly religious function. Andrew Greeley, in his book *The Religious Imagination*, points out that our imaginations are shaped by the residue of pictures and images which are stored up as a result of our personal experiences and our encounter with the symbols and stories of our religious tradition. His research suggests that Catholics who have warm and positive images of God, Christ, Mary and afterlife are more likely to be living happy family lives, participating in the life of the Church and working on behalf of social justice. This reminds us not only of the centrality of our imagination but also of the importance of shaping it by positive religious experiences.

Our ability to imagine is indeed a mysterious power. It opens up layers of experience hidden from rational calculation and thus puts us in touch with the Holy Spirit who calls us to a fulfillment beyond all imagining.

Chapter Two
Attitudes

Achieving a Healthy Trust of Our Experience

A lot of energy since Vatican II has been spent trying to explain Christianity as an *adult* religion, one based not on childish obedience, but on enlightened understanding. But "adult Christianity" is neither a simple message to get across to others nor an easy goal to reach in our own lives.

In a complex and changing world, with its daily demands on our intelligence and freedom, the desire for a moral and spiritual refuge is understandably intensified. Religious training often responds to this genuine need for security with a distorted and infantile version of Christianity, which suggest that *one's own experience should not be trusted.*

According to this view, authority figures such as the infallible pope, the local pastor and the well-known theologians always know best what is to be believed or practiced. The clear message communicated is this: In the world of spiritual concerns, the experience, insights and judgments of others are more important than one's own. Better to listen passively and to accept obediently than to think for oneself and to act creatively. The payoff, of course, is that one is then able to inhabit the secure world of clear-cut morality, authoritarian structures and infallible dogmas.

The struggle to set aside this childish Christianity is not confined to middle-aged Catholics who grew up in the

21

pre-Vatican II Church. It is a continuing challenge for all persons who want their faith understanding to match their maturity level.

As persons move from childhood through adolescence to adulthood, they gradually learn to trust many aspects of their own experience. To attain personal wholeness, this trusting self-confidence must encompass the religious and moral realm as well. To remain in an infantile spiritual state undercuts and truncates the general maturation process. This distortion produces persons who are at home and confident in the everyday world of family, work and leisure, but who are diffident and unsure in the world of explicit religion.

Emerging from an infantile religious outlook to a more adult Christianity is a liberating experience. People talk about a newfound freedom and about the exhilaration of thinking for themselves. They enjoy trusting their intuitions and taking their emotions seriously.

"I am learning to trust my experience" is the phrase which captures this process. Some say it defiantly with unmistakable undertones of anger directed at those who have retarded their progress in the past. Some say it with wide-eyed enthusiasm, as though they were the first ones to discover this liberating approach. Some say it with a zealous evangelical tone, which indicates eagerness to spread the message to others. Finally, some say it with a quiet confidence that seems solid and realistic.

Whatever the tone, however, it is vital that progress in trusting our experience be balanced by other considerations and placed in a larger framework.

Our experience is ambivalent—a mixture of both constructive and destructive patterns. We are creatures of sin as well as grace. Our insights into our existence can be clouded and it is possible to misunderstand the meaning of our experience. We have our moments of oversight as well as insight. Our judgments can be faulty, based on insufficient evidence and subject to personal bias. We have all made false as well as true judgments. While "trusting experience" is an essential step in moving toward an adult spirituality it is not, as commonly understood, the definitive guiding principle.

One way to place this value of "trusting experience" in a more comprehensive framework is to locate ourselves within a supportive and challenging faith community. From this position we can see that our own experience is very limited and can be enriched by the diverse experiences of others. In this setting we can openly express our insights, thereby exposing them to the criticism of others. The faith community enables us to make better judgments about the meaning and direction of our lives by providing us with a rich tradition and a common value system.

To avoid an excessive individualism in trusting our experience, we must realize that *our self-experience is always communal, shaped by our interaction with others and dependent on larger systems of meaning.* If we could always keep this in mind, then "trusting experience" would be a more reliable guideline.

In reality, however, the thrill of escaping the domination of authority figures often leads to an excessively private understanding of experience. Trusting experience becomes a matter of listening to an inner voice that is often solitary and self-serving.

Any attempt to criticize the prevalent notion of trusting experience is unpopular and potentially troublesome. Many people today are interested in striving for an adult Christianity. Some are involved in a courageous struggle to overcome an excessively rigid training. Others are intoxicated with new freedom and not receptive to what sounds like a return to the imprisonment of the past.

Surely those climbing toward a more mature religious position need support and encouragement, especially since guilt and fear exert such a powerful downward pull. That climb is made more surely and realistically, however, if we have a proper notion of the ideal towards which we move.

That ideal could be expressed as a healthy combination of trusting *and mistrusting* our experience. We are at our best when we learn from our experience but recognize its limitations; when we are in touch with our emotions but realize they can be askew; when we value our intuitions but are willing to check them out; when we think for ourselves but subject our insights to the critique of others; when we decide our own course of action but in dialogue with the values of a larger community.

I believe this emphasis on both trusting and mistrusting experience, properly presented, will encourage the ascent toward greater spiritual maturity. Those who feel guilty about overthrowing an excessively authoritarian morality and belief system will be encouraged by a reminder that laws and doctrines continue to play a vital role in a more adult Christianity. Those struggling to gain a new freedom will come to a greater appreciation of their need for supportive community. Finally, all those experiencing the exhilaration of reaching the plateau of a private and individualistic freedom will realize that the climb is not ended. The path of adult Christianity continues toward a never-attained summit where "trusting experience" is in healthy tension with a sense of limitation and the need for others.

Learning Self-Acceptance

Self-acceptance is at the center of our efforts to be responsive to the presence of the Spirit. The more we can accept ourselves, the better we are able to love others. Furthermore, self-acceptance necessarily involves acceptance of God even if this correlation is not brought to consciousness or is denied. Thus the great Jesuit theologian Karl Rahner can insist that self-acceptance be seen as the whole of the spiritual life—the one thing necessary for salvation, the key to human growth, and the primary means for surrendering to the gracious mystery we call God.

This line of thought, of course, depends on a proper understanding of the self. It presupposes, first of all, that the self is *not an isolated entity* but a "being in the world." Of course that "world" is not merely a collection of isolated objects but an organic whole in which things exist for the sake of persons. The self therefore is essentially involved in an interpersonal world.

Human growth depends upon achieving loving mutuality in these relationships. Self-acceptance demands accepting in practice this mutual dependence. A reflective acceptance of self involves a conscious recognition that our spiritual development is necessarily linked with our ability to achieve loving personal relationships. In biblical terms, the love of self and the love of neighbor are essentially connected.

Second, a proper understanding of self presupposes that we are *essentially related to mystery*. This suggests that we are not merely a bundle of responses to stimuli, or clever animals which can be exhaustively understood by empirical analysis and logical deduction. On the contrary, our orientation to mystery means that we are dependent on a Power greater than ourselves and that we move toward a goal which transcends all finite realities. It means that we cannot understand ourselves as knowers apart from an Absolute Truth which enables us to know particular truths; nor can we appreciate our activity as lovers without an Absolute Good which energizes and lures our affective powers. The self is related to the Incomprehensible One who calls for both surrender and self-transcending activity.

Acceptance of ourselves as we really are demands accepting our dependence on the Mystery which both supports and draws us. In other words, *self-acceptance is the acceptance of God*. This remains true even if this relationship is repressed, forgotten or denied. In biblical terms we are called upon to love God with our whole mind, heart and soul—thus accepting wholeheartedly our creaturely orientation to the Gracious Mystery.

When we realize that the self is fundamentally related to others and through them to the Absolute Other, then the centrality of self-acceptance in the spiritual life becomes clearer. Accepting self implies accepting our need to love and be loved in the process of human development. It also implies accepting our contingency—that we do not control our existence, but receive it from the Power greater than ourselves.

Self-acceptance, rather than being an individualistic and isolated act, turns out to be a lifelong process carried out in dialogue with others and in dependence on the Mysterious One. To achieve greater self-acceptance is already to be a better lover of God and of neighbor.

How can we arrive at a deeper, more comprehensive acceptance of self? This is another way of asking how we can make progress in the spiritual life.

We can begin by gradually learning to accept various "givens" which, despite our best efforts, cannot be overcome: our limited intelligence; our disappointments in personal relationships; our frustration in not attaining our ideals; our unavoidable bodily deterioration; our being confined and limited by previous decisions; and our anxiety over death. In discovering how to live with our limitations, we are preparing for the more fundamental and comprehensive act of self-acceptance: total surrender to God.

When we stop protecting our self-interests and reserving our existence exclusively for ourselves, we gradually move toward a greater realism about ourselves. This culminates in the ultimate realism of accepting that we are not divine, but are oriented toward and dependent upon the true God.

Here are some steps we might take in this process of self-acceptance:

1) Practice facing a particular fear as a preparation for confronting the deeper anxiety that accompanies our sense of finitude.

2) Strive to be patient with our limited growth and maturation as part of a lifelong process of surrendering to God.

3) Place all future planning into the context of an essentially unknowable future so we can remain open to the surprising things God has in store for us.

4) Acquire the facility of calmly passing up many opportunities for personal development in order to learn that self-fulfillment ultimately comes from a proper relationship to God, not an accumulation of experiences.

5) Finally, work at facing and accepting our own death in order to prepare for that final and complete act of handing ourselves over to the Gracious Mystery.

Those who have consciously entered into this process know how difficult it is. Facing our personal demons scares us, and confronting our finitude produces the threat of being overtaken by nothingness. Being patient with ourselves makes us fearful of settling for mediocrity or losing our idealism. Realizing our need to enter into loving human relationships produces a fear of being swallowed up and sacrificing our autonomy. Recognizing the limitations of our ability to plan the future causes worry over the unknown and uncontrollable character of that future. Passing up opportunities for expanding our

experiences makes us anxious that we will miss something
important. Facing death heightens the anxiety produced by
meeting any of the limits of our existence.

Thus spiritual growth encounters great resistance because
self-acceptance comes hard and is never completed. Yet
self-acceptance is facilitated by explicitly recognizing the
gracious character of the mystery that surrounds us. It is easier
to let go of the pockets of self-sufficiency if we believe that the
process can be trusted—that the source of our life is friendly, that
the unknowable future is benign, that there is wholeness for our
fragmented existence, that there is fulfillment of our deepest
desires, that there is fullness of life after death. In short,
self-acceptance—which always involves implicit acceptance of
the divine source and goal—is aided by *explicit* belief in the
goodness of God.

Likewise our faith in the kindness of God can be
strengthened by successful, though partial, acts of
self-acceptance. We can think of times when, for example, we
truly accepted one of our limitations and found this liberating;
when we courageously faced a fear and discovered it to be less
powerful than we thought; when we fought anxiety by silent
meditation and felt an inner peace; when we fleetingly faced
death and experienced a surprising strength. Such experiences are
clues that the Power in control of our lives can be trusted.

Out of this interaction between belief in God and efforts
at self-acceptance, a process of spiritual growth emerges. Daily
we must struggle to achieve a total surrender to God and to
accept, one step at a time, the various limitations which
constitute our existence.

Looking for 'Miracles'

Our outlook on miracles reflects our general perception of the
way we relate to God. I have friends who seem to expect miracles

A Framework

to happen regularly. They are convinced of the miraculous power of prayer and speak easily of healings. For them Jesus Christ the healer is always present for those with sufficient faith.

Let me contrast this view with some thoughts of the Catholic fiction writer Flannery O'Connor, expressed in letters to her friends at the time of a trip to Lourdes in 1958.

Flannery was suffering from a terminal disease known as lupus, and was being urged by friends and relatives to use the baths at Lourdes in hope of a cure. With obvious resistance she remarked facetiously that she "was one of those people who could die for his religion easier than take a bath for it." Flannery insisted that she would go to Lourdes as a pilgrim and not a patient. A friend surmised that she was opposed to going into the baths because she dreaded the possibility of a cure in those circumstances.

Eventually, in order to please her relatives, she did go through the ritual of taking the bath and drinking the water. Later she wrote lightheartedly that she, of course, fully accepted the world of the supernatural, but that it displaced nothing of the natural except perhaps the germs in the common drinking cups at Lourdes. For her, the real miracle of Lourdes was the avoidance of serious epidemics despite the unsanitary conditions.

Flannery O'Connor, a woman of great faith and tremendous confidence in her Catholic heritage, died of lupus in 1964 at the age of 39. A brilliant writing career was tragically cut short. It seems she neither expected, nor even dared ask for, a miracle to save her life.

My friends and Flannery O'Connor represent two contrasting attitudes toward miracles which are found among good people today. Some speak easily of divine interventions and miraculous healings. They are confident that God can cure people through the power of prayer, that the Anointing of the Sick is a sacrament of physical healing. Other people facing illness speak more of accepting reality. They believe in a God who supports us in dealing with inevitable suffering. For them prayer is primarily an act of submission and the Anointing of the Sick a preparation for death. Thus we are able to discern two obviously diverse pieties founded on divergent theologies.

With these diverse spiritual outlooks in mind, let us examine again the New Testament understanding of miracles.

The Gospels clearly present Jesus as a man who performs marvelous deeds and goes about doing good to individuals in need. Both friend and foe thought of him as a miracle worker. He refuses, however, to work "legitimating" miracles—ones which would clearly prove his claim to be the final prophet. In fact, doing some spectacular deed such as jumping down from the top of the Temple to impress the crowds is presented as a temptation from the Evil One which Jesus decisively rejects.

The people of Jesus' time did not think of miracles as a breaking of the laws of nature nor did they find them totally foreign. Such mighty deeds performed by others besides Jesus fit into their general perception of the world. For these people, *the real problem was the continuing battle between the good God and the powers of evil.* The mighty deeds of Jesus were a sign to the people of faith that the power of good was at work, that the kingdom was being established, that the Evil One could be defeated. It was amazing to them that this unlikely fellow from Nazareth was the one leading the onslaught against the evil which threatened the reign of God.

There is a reticence about miracles in the New Testament. The marvelous signs of Jesus are presented without many of the spectacular elements which surrounded the reported actions of other miracle workers. The story of the cure of Peter's mother-in-law through a simple touch is a good example.

In Mark's Gospel there is the so-called "messianic secret" in which Jesus warns people not to tell others about his remarkable deeds. Mark does not want his community to concentrate on miracles while forgetting that the cross is an essential element in following Jesus. All of the evangelists avoid the usual Greek word for "miracle" and speak instead of Jesus "doing good" or "performing mighty deeds." These wondrous happenings really function as signs of the presence of God who struggles against human suffering—a great message of hope to the people of faith who knew well the battle with the powers of evil.

The relation between miracles and faith in the Gospels is not easy to unravel. Sometimes Jesus cures persons while insisting that their faith saved them. He could not work miracles in his hometown of Nazareth, perhaps because they thought of him as too ordinary or, more likely, because they identified his mighty deeds with the work of the Evil One as did many of the opponents of Jesus. At times, the miracles are presented as a challenge to the weak faith of his followers. The calming of the storm is described as a rebuke to the inconsistent faith of the disciples of Jesus who should have had a deeper trust in him. In the case of the centurion, it seems that the faith of the interceding soldier was sufficient for the cure of his sick servant who is not even in direct contact with Jesus. *Thus miracles seem to be both responses to faith and challenges to unbelief.*

For contemporary theology miracles occur when people of faith discern the abiding presence of God manifested in a striking way, in and through particular events. It is not really a matter of a distant God intervening periodically in response to magical prayers by breaking the laws of nature. Rather, *in miracles the ever-present Gracious Mystery is discerned by the believer as active in a striking way in the struggle against human suffering.* Thus miracles give us hope by reminding us that good is more powerful than all the forces of evil. They also sharpen our awareness of the mystery dimension of life by putting us on alert to the new and surprising things which can happen when we don't imprison ourselves in a self-contained humanism.

From these biblical and theological perspectives, we can return to our original examples. My friends' optimistic piety highlights the truth that indeed God is at work in our world and that a faith-filled receptivity is vital for appreciating the divine presence. Confident prayer puts one on alert for the signals of hope that are scattered throughout our everyday existence. It is precisely such tangible reminders of the eventual triumph of good which motivate some people to keep their spirits up while continuing to bear their burdens in life. We all can benefit from this optimistic piety as long as we can place it in an acceptable theological framework which precludes notions of magical interventions.

Flannery O'Connor represents a modern version of the messianic secret which plays down miracles in favor of finding God in the ordinary. This piety concentrates on accepting the fundamental ambivalence of human existence. The thrust is to face the harsh side of life and accept our personal limitations without falling into a paralyzing despair. We gain motivation by trusting that the Gracious Mystery, which is secretly at work now in the struggle against human suffering, will ultimately triumph. For some people this is the best faith stance for maintaining a hopeful spirit which fosters effective Christian living.

There is no need to reject either of these two outlooks on miracles. Each perspective offers valuable insights into our ever-mysterious relationship with God. If we recognize and understand our own approaches then we will be prepared to capitalize on their strengths and transform their weaknesses.

Facing the Future

Our attitude toward the future has great bearing on how we respond to the Spirit in the present moment. Today there are sincere Christians who believe that the final showdown between God and the Antichrist will occur in the near future. For them all the signs are present: an increased number of earthquakes, the establishment of the State of Israel in 1947, the expansion of the European Common Market, threats of war in the Middle East and the spread of Communism.

Concerns about the end of the world and its accurate forecast fall under the general heading of *millenarianism*. This movement, which expects the imminent end of the present age, puts great emphasis on the thousand years of peace mentioned in the Book of Revelation.

Millenarianism is often connected with biblical fundamentalism, although not all fundamentalists believe the end is near. The key belief for fundamentalists is biblical inerrancy. At times, therefore, they adopt nonliteral interpretations of the Bible in order to prove that the Scriptures are indeed free from all error. Fundamentalist explanations of the creation accounts, for example, interpret the word *day* symbolically as a geological age or extended epoch so that the teaching of Genesis can be squared with modern evolutionary theory.

Millenarianists, however, tend to be more literal in their

interpretation, especially of the apocalyptic language contained in the books of Daniel and Revelation. They are totally opposed to evolutionary theory which suggests that the world is gradually improving. From their perspective, the world is really getting progressively worse, moving rapidly toward the time when God will intervene decisively to smash the power of evil and to inaugurate the thousand years of peace. Millenarianists are, of course, also strongly opposed to modern biblical criticism since it insists that the apocalyptic literature is not a literal prediction of the exact way that the end of the world will occur.

This pervasive expectation that the Lord will return soon dominated the thinking of the early Church and has reappeared throughout history. One form of this view is found in the so-called "dispensationalism" taught by J. M. Darby (1800-1882) and C. I. Scofield, who published the very influential *Scofield Reference Bible* in 1909. They held that we live in the age of the Church which stands between two ages when God works with Israel.

This teaching gets very detailed: Christ will come again soon; the saints or genuine Christians will be snatched mysteriously up into heaven in what is called "the rapture"; and 144,000 converted Jews will become the main messengers of Christ in establishing the thousand years of peace throughout the world. A variant of this *pre*-millennial outlook in which Christ comes *before* the period of peace is a *post*-millenial position in which Christ will return only after the Antichrist has been subdued and the millennium has occurred.

In all cases, these predictions are based upon a literal reading of the apocalyptic literature, especially Chapter 20 of the Book of Revelation, which speaks of Satan being chained for a thousand years during which time the elect will reign with Christ. The millenarianists are captivated by the descriptions of the end-time in the apocalyptic literature. For them the signs of this approaching time are clearly manifested in the contemporary world.

How are we to react to this growing movement with its apocalyptic interpretation of history?

1) *We can learn something from their urgent sense of being on alert for the coming of Christ.* Jesus and the early Church definitely insisted that true disciples must always be

prepared for the arrival of the kingdom which comes like the thief in the night, when least expected. This suggests the need for a heightened sense of the presence of the Spirit which motivates us to Christianize the world. We must seize the moment to work for good because evil powers roam our earth.

The person who is properly on alert does not shirk responsibility by drifting through life but grabs hold by actively preparing for the coming of the kingdom. I know of one millenarianist who intends to become a missionary even though he is expecting the final judgment very soon. Thus the expectation of the return of the Lord need not cause paralysis but can, rather, motivate constructive action to spread the kingdom.

2) *We can ask millenarianists how they know more about the end of the world than Jesus does.* In Mark 13:32 Jesus says about the final judgment: "As to the exact day or hour, no one knows it, neither the angels in heaven nor even the Son, but only the Father."

This is, of course, to play the proof-texting game which is not, by itself, a legitimate use of Scripture since any individual verse must be interpreted in light of the whole of the Scripture. In this case, however, it does seem that Jesus did expect the coming of the kingdom to be imminent. This gets reflected in the belief of the first generation of Christians that Jesus would return very soon to complete his work. This verse in Mark may shock millenarianists into more serious thought about the validity of their literal interpretations of Scripture as well as their confident predictions of the future.

3) *We must point out that apocalyptic literature is really "crisis" literature written to people in a time of persecution to bolster their faith that the God who never abandons them will eventually accomplish the triumph of good over evil.*

The Book of Revelation was written, in its final form, near the end of the first century during the reign of Domitian, who was assassinated in 96 A.D. Since Christians were being persecuted at the time by the Romans, the author used symbolic language borrowed from his Jewish tradition to strengthen their faith and resolve. He did not intend to predict events that would occur 2,000 years later. Can we really imagine an author in that crisis situation writing about the expansion of the European Common Market?

A Framework

The numbers used are not literal but symbolic. The visions recorded are not strict predictions of future details but a literary device to bring out the message of hope. All attempts to relate the Book of Revelation to current signs are simply misguided from the beginning. All those throughout history who have used it to predict the exact time of the end of the world—and there have been many—have been wrong. There is no reason to give any more credibility to our contemporary prophets of doom.

4) *We need to be aware of the emotional factors involved in a millenarianist outlook.* What psychological needs are met by having a firm grasp on the future? How is the drive for security connected with the assurance that one will be snatched up with the saints in "the rapture"? What deeper needs are met by knowing one is in the light and others are in the darkness?

It is true that there is an emotional component in all belief systems, but it is still beneficial to recognize the distinct patterns operative in the millenarianist. One possible factor is the need to control the intense anxiety produced by an unknown and uncertain future. Claims of knowing when the end will come, understanding the inner secrets of the divine plan, and having assurance of personal salvation can create a comfortable, if false, security.

We should not minimize the terror which an unknown future can produce. In dialogue with those who base their peace of mind on *control* of the future, we can suggest by word and example that genuine security in the face of anxiety is based on trust in a God who faithfully and lovingly guides us into an essentially unknowable future.

Chapter Three
The Dialectical Virtues

Cultivating a Reflective Spontaneity

When we live spontaneously and immerse ourselves in the present moment we are more likely to discern the intimations of the presence of the Spirit. We are, however, often distracted and removed from our immediate experience.

We can all think of times when we attended an event such as a concert or play and found our minds wandering and our hearts unsettled. We tried to concentrate but extraneous images and fleeting thoughts paraded through our minds. Then suddenly we found ourselves absorbed again in the activity at hand without any conscious effort on our part. Such experiences point to an important attribute for the spiritual search which I call "reflective spontaneity." The phrase suggests a paradoxical union of two apparent opposites in an integrated synthesis.

We want to participate wholeheartedly in the events of our lives but need insight and understanding to do so. It is desirable to live in a self-forgetful way, but this requires self-awareness. We want to be attentive to our current experience, but this seems to be facilitated by regular meditation. Our ideal, therefore, should be to combine a spontaneous immersion in the present moment with periodic self-examination which in turn frees us to live fully in the now.

There are at least two types of obstacles to achieving this ideal. The first is *an exclusive preoccupation with self.*

A Framework

We can't live spontaneously when we are continually examining our motives, wondering if we are pleasing others, worrying about our image and checking our relationship with the deity. Our culture seems to intensify this natural human tendency to turn in on ourselves. Historically we have been influenced by a Calvinistic Protestantism which puts great stress on recognizing both our personal guilt and our inner need for the grace of the sovereign God. For a couple of decades we have seen a proliferation of self-help books, heard the message to get in touch with our deeper feelings and sensed the call to plumb the depths of our own psyche. Even theology has responded to this trend by adopting autobiographical methods (such as helping us become better readers of the stories we necessarily author) and analyzing the imaginative and emotional side of religious experience.

I have taken advantage of this trend myself by teaching courses on religious self-awareness which invite students to become more aware of the deeper dimensions of their own experience by wrestling with the great human questions. Collegians who are naturally involved in a process of self-discovery find this approach both attractive and useful.

Cultural trends which produce excessive preoccupation with ourselves make genuinely spontaneous living difficult. But an even more prevalent obstacle to a reflective spontaneity is *the temptation to live without sufficient reflection.*

It is easy to get involved in the busyness of life and to fail to pause and reflect. We sometimes allow life to become like a rat race in which there is no chance to stop and gain perspective. It is possible to live on the surface of life without descending into the depths of the soul. Material things can dominate our attention and leave no room for the spiritual. The cares of the day can dull our taste for the infinite. The press of problems can submerge our sense of mystery. We can become so busy that we miss the friendship of others, the joys of family life and the perspective of prayer.

In summary some people find themselves ensnared by a guilt-ridden, paralyzing preoccupation with self while others live a busy, unexamined life in which the law of diminishing returns takes over.

Rather than swinging between these two extremes we must strive for a life of reflective spontaneity in which our reflection makes wholehearted living possible. We can begin by recognizing which element we are in danger of diminishing or eliminating—spontaneity or reflection. With this in mind we can work to restore a productive interaction between the two.

For example, a girl came to me preoccupied with continual doubts about her motivations and with nagging questions about the appropriateness of her actions. I encouraged her to bracket these problems by writing them down and limiting her consideration of them to a brief discussion with me once a week. This simple technique seemed to free her to live with greater spontaneity in her daily life as she gradually learned to deal with her doubts.

Persons suffering from an excessive self-consciousness are sometimes helped by discerning the imagined audience for which they generally perform. Parents and respected peers are good possibilities. Healing often occurs when a person decides that continually performing for someone else does not make sense. This allows more spontaneous, inner-directed behavior to emerge.

Those of us in danger of eliminating the reflective side of the dialectic often need more systematic approaches. We need, for example, to meditate regularly and to spend time in prayer and spiritual reading each day. An improved prayer life will help attune us to the mystery of life and clarify our values.

We must, of course, each find our own precise rhythm in these matters. Some individuals, for example, find 15 minutes of meditation a day, one day of leisure a week, Confession every six months and an annual retreat just about right. Others would not function well with this pattern. We all have to do the amount and type of reflecting that sufficiently focuses our attention, quiets our heart and offers perspective on our experience. Our goal is to hear the God who speaks to us in and through the series of *present* moments which constitute our life.

Striving for a Committed Openness

In order to attune ourselves to the Spirit, we need to cultivate a healthy, open-minded attitude. This involves a continual struggle to avoid both a *mindless relativism* which thinks that one idea or value is as good as another as well as an *exclusive attitude* which automatically denies truth and goodness to those who think differently. Thus, we should strive for the ideal of *committed openness* in which we are receptive to truth, goodness and beauty precisely because we are rooted in a particular tradition and confident of our own standpoint.

Important strides in the direction of a healthy openness were made as a result of Vatican II's emphasis on respect for the beliefs and practices of other religions or humanistic traditions.

While Church leaders and theologians carry on ecumenical dialogues internationally, members of local congregations have the opportunity to meet in interfaith settings to pray and solve social problems. In the United States this openness is supported by our tradition of democratic pluralism. Nevertheless, the solidity of these gains remains questionable. For some, the ghetto of religious narrowness has been replaced by an amorphous world lacking intellectual roots and moral convictions. An undergraduate student with healthy universalist sentiments, for example, told me that she is confused because her roommate keeps insisting that only explicit Christians can be saved. A traditional Catholic reported that while he really does believe non-Catholics will be saved, he can't square this with what he was taught in school. A woman asked me what she is supposed to say to her charismatic friend who insists there is no salvation except in explicitly calling upon the name of the Lord Jesus.

It is as if the modern movement rejecting the old

exclusivism has produced its own backlash. The anxiety accompanying newfound freedom sends some back to the safe rigidity of a narrow particularism. The mindlessness of some universalists reinforces a reactionary dogmatism in others. The inability of some more open individuals to justify their position encourages a smug complacency among those still inhabiting the religious ghetto.

Such resurgent exclusivism is understandable, but it must be fought. Religious exclusivism can hurt individuals and communities, justify cruelty to others, and sow the seeds of discord. The Holocaust and its connection with religious prejudice should not be allowed to fade from our consciousness. The religious strife in Northern Ireland, the proliferation of cults and the exclusivist tendencies in the charismatic renewal are reminders of these dangers.

One weapon in the fight against religious exclusivism is the ability to give a rational vindication of a more universalist position.

On the one hand, it is true that there is a long and consistent position in Christian thought which clearly states that there is no salvation outside the Church. For example, Pope Boniface VIII in *Unam Sanctam* (1302) stated: "We declare, say, define and pronounce that it is absolutely necessary for the salvation of every human creature to be subject to the Roman Pontiff." It is also true that there are many restrictive statements in the New Testament. The Gospels do proclaim, for instance, that Jesus is the way, the truth and the life.

On the other hand, Vatican II stated: "Those also can attain to everlasting salvation who through no fault of their own do not know the gospel of Christ or His Church, yet sincerely seek God and, moved by grace, strive by their deeds to do His will as it is known to them through the dictates of conscience. Nor does Divine Providence deny the help necessary for salvation to those who without blame on their part, have not yet arrived at an explicit knowledge of God, but who strive to live a good life, thanks to His grace" (*Lumen Gentium*, #16).

How are we to explain this striking contrast in official statements which move from the narrowest exclusivism demanding explicit adherence to the pope for salvation to the broadest universalism envisioning the salvation even of atheists?

A Framework

Among other things, our understanding of Church dogma must include the idea that doctrines are historically conditioned. The Church only gradually grows in her understanding of the teachings of Jesus. Thus the Church of Vatican II, influenced by contemporary insights such as the unity of the human community and the dignity of all individuals, has arrived at a more comprehensive interpretation of the universality of Christ's redemption than was possible in the time of Boniface VIII.

As the Church grows in understanding, she refocuses on important elements in her tradition. Thus, universalist notions in the Scriptures are highlighted. Think of the satire on Jewish exclusiveness in the Book of Jonah and the "light of the nations" theme in Isaiah. Recall the prologue to John's Gospel which indicates that the Word enlightens *all* human beings, as well as the salvation theology that Christ takes away the sins of the whole world (1 John 2:2) and that the Father wills the salvation of all (1 Timothy 2:4-6). From this perspective Peter was able to say that "the man of any nation who fears God and acts uprightly is acceptable to him" (Acts 10:35).

This refocusing extends to our theological tradition as well. To pick just one striking example: Justin Martyr, who in the middle of the second century taught that the *Logos* was operative in all people, thought of good people such as Socrates as Christians (an early version of the "anonymous Christian" notion). This line of thought can be traced from Clement of Alexandria in the period of the Fathers, through Bonaventure in the Middle Ages to Karl Rahner in our own time.

To solidify the universalist perspectives of Vatican II, we need a theological rationale which shows how even atheists can have salvific faith. Here is a possible outline of such a theology:

God wills the salvation of all human beings (1 Tm 2:4-6). To this end God gives himself to all people (grace). This self-communication makes a difference in people, giving them the ability to respond to God and modifying their consciousness. The presence of God in the heart of all those who are open to his grace produces a type of revelation which is manifested in the call of conscience, the impulse to do good and the appreciation of goodness. When persons respond honestly to this universal revelation, they are acting with faith which moves them toward salvation. Thus an individual can be saved by meeting responsibilities, loving others and following the dictates of conscience even though there is no explicit recognition of God, Christ or Church.

This brief outline of a theology of salvation would, of course, have to be filled in with explanations and argumentation. It does, however, suggest an approach for vindicating universalism and fighting the growing religious exclusivism.

Developing a Hopeful Realism

An attitude of hopeful realism will help keep us alert to the mysterious workings of the Spirit. This virtue prompts mature believers to stay in touch with reality, including its dark and tragic dimension, while at the same time retaining an ultimate hope in the triumph of good over evil. This outlook must be at the core of all genuine Christian piety which knows both the Cross and the Resurrection.

The Christian ideal is to accept the fundamental ambivalence of life with confidence that the saving work of God will not finally be frustrated. This ideal, which is obviously easier to state than to live, stands in contrast to two other extreme positions—*naive optimism* and *cynical pessimism*. For the most part, we experience these extremes not as total viewpoints, but as tendencies or temptations within ourselves and others.

A naive optimist refuses to face the darkness of human existence, escapes from the tension involved in the struggle between good and evil, abhors talk of limitations, and rules out the tragic dimension of life. Examples of this tendency are not hard to find even in our sometimes cynical modern world: the conviction that all human problems are solvable, that life is essentially fair, that the United States can still police the world on behalf of good, that science can assure continual progress and even that death can be overcome by technical means such as freezing bodies.

A Framework

In the realm of religion, the temptation of naive optimism also threatens: when people speak of resurrection without the cross, when cheap grace prevails and sin is put into a zone of silence, when instant conversions remove the need for continual effort, when the latest spiritual technique is put forward as a panacea and when talk of the dark night of the soul is perceived as violating Christian joy.

The tone of this naively optimistic spirituality is evident in statements such as: "My wallet has been stolen—Praise the Lord"; "I failed my exam—God is good"; "The relationship broke up—Thank you, Jesus." I suppose such phrases could represent a healthy and even heroic outlook. For many, however, they sound hollow, escapist and unrealistic. When the authentic human emotions of anger, disappointment, frustration and sadness are repressed, the victory is too easy, the spirituality too saccharine.

Cynical pessimists on the other hand are so immersed in the heaviness of life and so overwhelmed by evil that they cannot rise above it, or see any way out. Perhaps we do not find many pure types outside the novels of Camus and the plays of Beckett. But surely the temptation to cynicism is real enough today: "Everyone in government is corrupt"; "You can't trust anyone anymore"; "It is impossible to make marriage work"; "My faults cannot be overcome, there is no sense trying anymore"; "Nuclear destruction is inevitable"; "The Fates are against me."

In this view, evil reigns supreme and the potential for good is denied. Life is ultimately absurd because there is "no exit," no way to illumine the darkness, no context of meaning within which evil can be placed. There may be a few heroes who can live effectively with this outlook, but for most it is paralyzing and deadening.

In a world which swings between naive optimism and cynical pessimism, we must strive to understand and live out a *hopeful realism*. Such realism involves facing life in all its ambiguity, accepting the inevitable struggle between good and evil, learning to cope with the full range of our emotions, acknowledging our strengths as well as our limitations, affirming life and death, and celebrating both the cross and the resurrection.

Facing the negative side of life is just too frightening for many people. They fear that such a confrontation would induce a perpetual blue mood, upset psychic equilibrium and eventually destroy them.

Nevertheless, the essential truth of life must be maintained: *There is no other way to wholeness except by incorporating the dark side.* Demons once faced have less power than when left lurking in the shadows. The cross leads to resurrection.

The hope which overcomes cynical pessimism is finally based on a faith that is reasonable but which transcends empirical analysis and logical deduction. It involves the conviction that the process of life can be trusted, that absurdity fits into a larger context of meaning, that the good will prove stronger than evil in the long run. We can bear grief because we believe the tears will be wiped away one day. We can continue the struggle because we believe all human effort is finally worthwhile. We can face our sins and weaknesses because we believe in a God who loves us.

In order to maintain faith in God's ultimate victory we must find signals of hope in our everyday experience. We might consider the times when we fought the demons and were not destroyed; when we admitted a weakness and made progress; when we faced a crisis and discovered surprising strength; when we suffered through depression and emerged with a lighter spirit; when we confronted death and felt hope enkindled. Such experiences can be seen as intimations that an absolute pessimism is unwarranted and that a friendly power is at work.

Within this hopeful realism there is a tendency to emphasize either the hope or the realism. There are some people who are more optimistic, tend to look on the brighter side of life, are attuned to the signals of hope and sense the gracious presence of God. They are excited by the possibility of personal growth and energized by the hope of human progress. This "springtime piety" has been well represented in our own century by Teilhard de Chardin, the Jesuit scientist and religious visionary.

There are others who are more pessimistic, tending to notice the darker side of life. They are sensitive to the finitude of human existence and struggle with the apparent absence of God. The world appears to them, in historical perspective, as a rather constant mix of good and evil. The Jesuit theologian Karl Rahner represents this outlook.

A Framework

Rahner describes his own piety as 'wintry,' formed by the icy blasts of an often harsh and cruel world. His famous book of prayers, appropriately entitled *Encounters With Silence* (or, if literally translated, *Words Into Darkness*), responds to the inadequacy of verbalized prayer and the lack of a clear divine response. He thinks that contemporary Christians must develop a *sober realism* which appreciates the bitterness of life, the radical risk of human existence and the threat of sin and guilt. He insists that *everything which blossoms must pass through death.*

The cross is our constant reminder that we dare not dishonestly suppress the hardness of life nor take refuge from reality in the opiate of easy joy and cheap grace. This kind of realism is made possible only by hope in the power of God to bring about a better and more fulfilling future. This hope in turn frees us to appreciate the joys of the world, to open ourselves to reality, to work to spread peace and justice, to fulfill our limited potential.

Some think that this Rahnerian spirituality will lead to paralysis and despair. I think, on the contrary, it has great potential to liberate us for constructive action. If we accept that a proposed project will not be the greatest, then we are free to pursue it. If we acknowledge the continuing presence of prejudice, then we are moved to a long-term commitment to combat it. If we accept the boundary set by our own death, then we are inspired to make the most of the time given us. If we admit our sins, we are in a position to seek forgiveness. In general when we admit our limitations, we sense in a deeper way the need to hand over our lives to the God who alone can save us.

Overcoming the Eclipse of Mystery

A common problem for our modern Western culture is the eclipse of mystery. The deeper, more significant dimensions of life are often obscured, distorted or forgotten because we lead busy and distracted lives in a culture which emphasizes the superficial and the trivial. In order to preach the gospel effectively we must first recover the sense of mystery. As a first step it is helpful to bring into conscious awareness the deeper aspects of particular experiences which often go unnoticed. We then are in a position to relate this heightened personal awareness to the meanings contained in particular Christian doctrines.

Let me fill out this abstract explanation by describing a five-step process I use in workshops or retreats.

1) *Recall and write down in vivid detail a significant encounter with another person.* This may be a personal interaction which involved high emotions or produced important results or just seemed to carry a deeper meaning despite its ordinariness.

I can recall, for example, the time my mother asked me to speak to my father about his driving habits which had become careless. I waited for a chance when we were alone. After suggesting with some trepidation that he should pay more attention to the road when he was driving, I stood back to catch the full force of his anger. With great passion he reminded me that my driving record wasn't all that great and that he could do without advice from his son on this matter. The next moment, with his wrath expended and the matter over with once and for all, he put his arm around my shoulders and began talking calmly and warmly about the possibilities of our annual summer fishing trip.

2) *Analyze the experience in terms of the ideals of human love*. Genuine love demonstrates certain characteristics: an effort to reach out to the beloved despite the temptation to selfishness; a mutuality in which each gives and receives trust and support; a respect for the individuality of the other which encourages uniqueness and personal development.

Elements of these ideals appear in my own example: my acceptance of my father's volatile personality; his gesture of putting his arm around my shoulder as a sign of reconciliation; our long-established mutual trust which made possible the straightforward honesty of the encounter.

This second step in the process sets up some ideal standards by which we can judge the quality of our ordinary experiences. It also directs our attention to the kind of love which characterizes the best of our human relationships.

3) *Examine this particular encounter for intimations of mystery*. This is a search for signals of transcendence, for clues that reveal the depth dimension of the interaction, for indications that this was a type of religious experience. It may help to keep in mind that religious experience is not necessarily extraordinary. Even our ordinary self-experience necessarily involves a religious dimension because it is empowered by a mysterious goal which lovingly allures us. God reveals himself to us in and through the simple events of life.

Appreciating religious experience demands the ability to see light in the darkness, the extraordinary in the ordinary. People vary both in the quality of their response to the mystery and in their ability to express the depths of their experience. But the presence of God remains an inescapable element in all human activity. Sometimes the experience seems mostly positive, as when we feel close to and in tune with the mystery; at other times it seems predominantly negative, as when we have a strong sense of our limitations and realize we are called to submit to a higher power.

In reflecting on the encounter with my father, I can discern the presence of mystery as I met and accepted my own limitations. In an even more striking way the mystery appeared as gracious as my father put his arm around my shoulders in a reconciling gesture.

4. *Try to find a good image of the mystery present in the encounter.* It may help to begin by describing the invisible power at work and looking for an image or symbol which collects the major points. This image based in experience can then be related to one of the traditional symbols of God found in the Bible.

We should remember that no one image *exhausts* the divine reality and that any particular image can be misleading. A good symbol grows out of our subjective experience of mystery and has the power to name the mystery, to express our commitment to it and to stir up our sense of its continuing presence.

In my example, the mystery shining in and through my father appears on the one hand as demanding, serious and worthy of respect. At the same time the mystery reveals itself as warm, compassionate and reconciling. No doubt, many similar experiences throughout my life have shaped my image of God as the loving source who demands respect. For me the *Abba* ("daddy") image used by Jesus is combined with a picture of the Majestic One who expects respect and fidelity.

This method of arriving at an image of God has the advantage of rooting our symbolic understanding of the deity in our experience, thereby ensuring that it is our own and not merely received from others.

5) *Relate the encounter to a particular biblical story.* We can begin by identifying biblical characters who underwent similar experiences or stories which portray similar encounters with God. Prayerful meditation on this scriptural material will reveal connections which illumine our experience. In my case, I think first of Isaiah's great inaugural vision in the Temple (Is 6:1-13). Yahweh seated on a high throne appears as the majestic Lord. The foundations of the Temple tremble with the divine presence. Isaiah, sensing his unworthiness, still manages to respond, "Here I am. Send me."

With equal vigor but greater comfort the Gospel story of the prodigal son also presses on my consciousness (Lk 15:11-32).

A Framework

The picture of the father running out and embracing his son strikes responsive chords within me. Together the two stories help me to understand in greater depth not only my encounter with my father but also the religious flavor of my daily experience.

In summary, the essence of this five-step process is to discern and name the Mystery lurking in our ordinary experience so that we can achieve an authentic appropriation of our Christian tradition.

Rediscovering Sin

The topic was *sin*. The unlikely setting was our monthly faculty gathering at which we take turns offering presentations on a topic reflecting our current interests or research. This time a sociologist presented us with a contemporary sociological profile of a healthy religious personality, pointing out how deficient that description was in terms of sin and guilt. By way of illustration he summarized the views of child psychologist Bruno Bettelheim and psychotherapist Karl Menninger.

Bettelheim insisted that children are deprived of a valuable way of dealing with their own impulses when fairy tales are sanitized by removing the portrayals of the villains and their demise. Menninger in his book *Whatever Became of Sin* claimed that we suffer from a vague anxiety when talk of sin is silenced. He castigated liberal clergy for intensifying this problem by refusing to talk about sin. When individuals reduce sin to neurosis and refuse to take responsibility for their blameworthy actions, they are no longer in a position to understand the real roots of anxiety or to make improvements in their lives.

With these fundamental ideas in front of us we began a general discussion.

• An educational theorist, greatly influenced by

Abraham Maslow, noted that his students often described themselves as "sinners." He quickly added, however, that he did not consider himself one and in fact had no idea what "being a sinner" might mean.

• A theologian reminded us that, while the popular notion of sin is breaking God's law, the Bible understands sin more in terms of a general condition of humankind than as individual transgressions.

• A professor with a strong humanities background began by admitting that religion in the abstract is supposed to produce healthy attitudes. She continued, however, by noting that in her actual experience, religion usually produced unhealthy guilt feelings through its emphasis on sin.

• A psychologist wanted to know what could possibly be gained by reintroducing all the negative images and emotions connected with the traditional notions of sin.

• A historian suggested that talk of sin made sense in the homogeneous and settled world of the Middle Ages where God's will was known through agreed-upon moral laws: In that culture sin was a clear violation of the commonly accepted norms of behavior. He wondered, however, if our pluralistic, secularized world today, with its confusion over moral standards, could really support any authentic understanding of sin.

Along with these comments which seemed to call any "sin-talk" into question, a number of responses spoke of the positive values of reintroducing sin in the context of personal experience.

• An expert in Romance languages said that scientific categories and empirical analyses were unable to penetrate the core of his own mysterious self-understanding which was strongly influenced by the Catholic sense of the reality of sin.

• A philosopher described in moving terms his own struggle with mental illness which included a couple of months in therapy with a psychiatrist. At one point he told the doctor that the understanding of his problems that emerged from the therapy was really not enough. In addition, he had to admit his wrongdoing, deal with his personal responsibility and come to grips with the mysterious depths of his own heart. The philosopher went on to describe his tremendous frustration with the psychiatrist who had no room for the category of "sin" in his own theoretical framework. This psychiatrist, according to the ironic comment of the philosopher, deserved the name 'shrink' because he was so insistent on *shrinking* the full range of his patients' experiences. *Sin had been shrunk to neurosis and the possibility of genuine healing denied.*

Throughout this fascinating discussion, I found myself thrilled by the heightened emotional tone and inspired by the very personal responses. The topic of sin—supposedly relegated to a zone of silence, especially in the enlightened world of Academe—had burst forth with surprising insistence. Indeed, talk of sin seemed to bring us close to the very core of what it means to be human.

Menninger was clearly right in suggesting that we are impoverished when sin becomes a taboo topic. Something deep and central remains unarticulated when the therapeutic mentality takes over and life is thought of only in terms of neurotic tendencies or an unimpeded process of self-actualization.

Let me reflect on this discussion from a theological perspective. It is indeed harder to talk of sin today because the medieval world has broken down, calling into question the eternal verities and the traditional moral laws. There is no denying the negative framework and repressive tone that accompanied the teaching of sin in the past. Surely there is danger today of unnecessarily reviving neurotic guilt feelings in people. Nevertheless, many people today are questioning the total abandonment of the language of sin because they believe our massive social evils result, at least in part, from a lack of personal responsibility. Some conservative Christians, as well as cultural critics, want to return to the "old-time" religion. A rigid, uncompromising Christianity, they believe, can again be the glue to hold society together. Strong talk of a judging God and the dangers of human sin can produce good citizens who will toe the line, work hard and avoid too much pleasure-seeking. A good dose of "sin-talk" will help save our American way of life.

It seems to me, however, that the contemporary world needs something besides a new barrage of heavy moralism on the one hand and a total abandonment of the talk of sin on the other. Neither the revival of traditionalist religion nor the contemporary therapeutic society offers us much hope.

I would look instead for illumination and transforming power from a reinterpretation of traditional Christian teachings on sin. Such a reinterpretation might go something like this:

The truth is that we live an ambivalent existence which is always a mix of good and evil, triumph and failure, virtue and vice. We deny or repress the negative side at our own peril.

There is a longstanding and enduring flaw which infects our heart and permeates our world. We know the inner temptation to violate conscience as well as the external forces which allure us toward destructive behavior. We Christians attribute this flaw to an original and continuing human rebellion against a loving God and name it, perhaps misleadingly, "original sin."

It is possible to view the physical evil involved in this flawed situation as an inevitable by-product of the process of God bringing a material, evolving moral world back to total union with himself.

In a world codetermined by good and evil, we *can* culpably choose the side of evil by refusing to love, by spreading disharmony, by escaping from reality, by being selfish, by acting destructively, by hurting others. We call such choices "personal sins." In committing them, we involve ourselves in the self-contradiction of turning against the very source of our freedom. Furthermore, we run the danger of developing destructive patterns in our personality which will continue to undermine our efforts to live virtuous lives.

Historically, personal sins have increased the pool of evil by creating unjust social systems and establishing oppressive institutions. Today we are more conscious of such systemic evil and call it "social sin."

Facing original, personal and social sin does not have to be a paralyzing and depressing experience. It can, in fact, be liberating. Facing sin puts us in touch with reality, enables us to improve ourselves and moves us to work for social justice. When this occurs we know the truth of the scriptural teaching that where sin exists, grace does more abound (Rom 5:21).

Dealing With Fundamentalists

The rise of religious fundamentalism has created a new set of problems for people interested in spiritual growth. The great emphasis among fundamentalists on striking religious experiences has caused many good people to feel that their own experiences of God are inferior. Some Christians have responded by compulsively seeking extraordinary encounters with the deity. Others withdraw into silence and give up the search for a deeper relationship with Christ.

I recall a particular encounter with a young fundamentalist. He was a little early for his appointment. He entered breezily with Bible in hand, beginning with a bit of small talk. Then in rapid fire he told the story of his recent conversion, pulled out a few proof texts to buttress his conviction that we are near the day of judgment, implied that my preaching was not representing the full gospel, and assured me that he would pray for me. This interchange has a familiar ring for many people today. It prompts some thoughts on how to deal more effectively with biblical fundamentalists.

1) *We need to be aware of our negative emotional reactions* to such encounters. Do we experience withdrawal, anger, defensiveness or frustration? What causes such responses? Are we upset because genuine dialogue seems impossible? Or does the enthusiasm of fundamentalists make our own approach seem inferior? Insight into our emotional responses can be a first step in acquiring the self-confidence needed for more fruitful exchanges with fundamentalists.

2) *It helps to realize that some fundamentalists are open to aspects of modern biblical criticism.* For example, 300 fundamentalists meeting in 1978 under the auspices of the International Council on Biblical Inerrancy produced the

so-called Chicago Statement. This document states that, in interpreting the Bible, "we must pay the most careful attention to its claims and character as a human production." It goes on to say that, in the Scriptures, "history must be treated as history, poetry as poetry, hyperbole and metaphor as hyperbole and metaphor" and that "differences between literary conventions in Bible times and ours must also be observed" (cf. J. I. Parker, *Beyond the Battle for the Bible*, p. 58). These rather surprising statements could provide a basis for dialogue with some fundamentalists. Often they are unaware of the currents of thought within their own circles.

3) *For some fundamentalists, biblical inerrancy provides a sense of security in a complex and changing world.* They claim absolute inerrancy in order to preserve the Bible's role as the authoritative guide for all beliefs and practices. It is easier to cope with life if all the answers are contained in one book, especially when the book is the infallible word of God.

In responding to fundamentalists it is important to appreciate the intensity of this drive for assurance and certitude. At the same time it is helpful to question whether absolute inerrancy can be maintained in the face of modern criticism. Furthermore, we should ask whether inerrancy is a truly effective means of achieving security in the contemporary world. In this discussion we should not give the impression that all we have to offer is more complexity and confusion. We should insist, rather, on the power of the Scriptures to help form a supportive community which can aid us in living faithfully despite the unavoidable ambiguity of our world.

4) *Raising obvious problems involved in a literal reading of the Scriptures can be legitimate and occasionally helpful.* How could there have been light before the creation of the sun as the Book of Genesis teaches? After the birth of Jesus, was he taken to Nazareth as in Luke or to Egypt as in Matthew? The purpose of such questions is to challenge the naive acceptance of literal interpretations of the Bible. Furthermore, it offers the opportunity to demonstrate the value of modern critical approaches which emphasize the *religious* truth contained in the Bible rather than the claim to scientific and historical truth.

5) *We should acknowledge the weaknesses as well as the strengths of modern biblical criticism.* On the positive side, the

insistence already noted—that the Bible teaches religious truth and not necessarily scientific or historical truth—enables us to deal with the disputes between science and religion. Clarification of the intentions of the author can enrich our appreciation of the way the Scriptures respond to real human problems. An understanding of literary forms helps us to concentrate on the essence of the saving message. The interest generated by modern approaches has produced a growing number of people engaged in Bible study and private reading.

At the same time, however, contemporary biblical scholars have themselves criticized the historical-critical method. Some have pointed to its tendency to focus on a scientific and historical analysis while ignoring the meaning of the text for the current community of faith. This may be a partial explanation for the negative reaction of fundamentalists when they encounter modern biblical criticism.

Another contemporary method of scriptural interpretation, often connected with the work of the philosopher Paul Ricoeur, tries to overcome these deficiences. This *structural* approach holds that the biblical text as we have it now has a life of its own beyond the intentions of the author and its original cultural setting. Thus, as we read the Bible today in the light of our current experience, it possesses a power to shatter our ordinary way of viewing reality and to open up new possibilities of living as a person of faith. This contemporary explanation of the "fuller sense" of Scripture may be a good basis for talking with fundamentalists who, with similar intent if less sophistication, are inclined to read the Bible for personal illumination.

6) *Explanations of the Bible should be placed in the context of our current experience.* The historical-critical method uncovers the human problems which the biblical authors were addressing as well as the faith perspective and the key insights they offered in response. This knowledge is helpful but not sufficient. We must go further by discerning similar concerns in our own time and culture and by working out contemporary expressions of biblical teachings which respond to these current concerns.

In other words, explaining Scripture is going to be more effective today if we make sure that the biblical message is responding to genuine questions raised by our culture. We must show how Scripture illumines our present struggles by suggesting more constructive patterns of living. Our task is to open up the meaning of the Bible so that it can supply energy for our efforts to humanize our world by disclosing to us the true source of our motivation and strength.

7) *Contemporary explanations of inspiration must clearly recognize the indispensable work of the Spirit.* This is crucial so that the modern approaches do not appear as a self-contained humanism but rather demonstrate an openness to the divine. We should remember that the modern form of biblical fundamentalism arose at the beginning of this century as a response to the fear that modern criticism was undermining the power of God's Word by reducing the Bible to a merely human book.

Since the Bible itself alludes to the rule of the faith community in the production of the Scripture (Lk 1:1-4), we must reject a dictation theory of inspiration whereby the human author functions merely as a recording secretary for God. On the other hand we must highlight the work of the Spirit in the whole of the believing community, especially in the final author who gathered the traditions in order to respond to the needs of the community.

Modern biblical criticism flows from an open-ended humanism which does not put God and human beings in competition. This suggests an account of the origin of the Scriptures which stresses God working in and through the human community as well as an understanding of authorship which recognizes the workings of the Spirit while respecting the unique contributions of the human authors.

Some of us find dialogue with fundamentalists quite difficult, but this does not absolve us from the responsibility of improving our approaches. Most of all, we must continue to trust our own types of religious experiences. We need not be overwhelmed by claims of clear-cut, striking experiences of the Lord. After all, in the Scriptures the Lord is present in subtle ways and in ordinary events such as encountering the needy and experiencing the gentle breeze.

Handling Complexity

In the midst of complexity we need a spirituality which is simple. As accelerating change sends out its bewildering signals, we long for a stable point which provides security. When we travel the dark path of grief and sorrow, there is need for clear reminders of hope and purpose. If the demon named "depression" begins to attack, our indispensable weapon is the simple conviction that it is manageable. When multiple pressures assail our self-confidence, the single notion that we are loved is sustaining. In the midst of competing moral demands we look for solid principles to guide our decision-making. As escapism in all its subtle guises tempts us, the need for a compelling motive for facing reality becomes more imperative. When a surprising array of factors coalesces to bring us joy and peace, simple words of gratitude seem most appropriate. Thus various common experiences remind us that, as the complexity of our lives increases, the need for *simple* faith responses becomes more urgent.

Modern complications, however, make the achievement of such a simple spirituality extremely difficult. The sum total of human experience and knowledge has become so vast that no one science or intellectual discipline can systematize or integrate it.

We also have to contend with a bewildering array of competing worldviews and philosophies. Eastern religions, Marxism, atheism and secularism—all provide viable alternatives to traditional outlooks. Classic scholastic philosophy is challenged and often replaced by linguistic analysis, existentialism, process thought or pragmatism. Many individuals find that their Christian faith can no longer adequately synthesize all aspects of life nor achieve the status of a totally comprehensive system.

In a previous age Christianity could more easily perform this integrating function because it held together a homogeneous culture in which a comprehensive religious outlook was simply taken for granted. With the demise of Christendom, this structure collapsed. Our culture is now shaped by competing forces because various worldviews are operative.

This objective situation makes it increasingly difficult for individuals to integrate completely their own experience, to reduce their knowledge to a comprehensive system and to understand the available insights of others. Since the culture no longer supplies a clear-cut, unified answer to the problems of human existence, the task of working out a viable personal philosophy is both taxing and subject to error.

In this situation skepticism may seem like the only intellectually honest response. Why commit ourselves to a cause or a moral position if it may some day be shown to be false? Some people judge it wiser to refuse to make explicit judgments about the deeper questions of life.

The complex character of our contemporary world, which many find so confusing and debilitating, underscores the current need for a simple spirituality based on a firm grasp of the essence of Christianity. One difficulty, though, is that the Christian faith itself often seems to be a mysterious complex of unconnected doctrines, arbitrary laws and unintelligible rituals. Working out a simple spirituality involves cutting through this complexity and uncovering for ourselves the very core of the Christian message.

Christianity, in fact, is a simple and unified response to the question of meaning and purpose which lurks at the very center of our being. It speaks to us the joyful news that good is stronger than evil, that love triumphs over hate, that the absurdities which threaten are actually encompassed by meaning and that our seemingly wasted efforts are abidingly worthwhile. In short, Christian faith proclaims that the sometimes frightening mystery which surrounds us is actually gracious and totally faithful.

These notions are not mere abstractions. Christianity points to the historical Jesus of Nazareth as the concrete expression of this loving concern. He is the parable of God's true nature revealing, by word and conduct, the absolutely trustworthy character of the Father. He has planted the seeds of final victory making irrevocable the ultimate triumph of the universal saving will of God. In Jesus, all of history finds its meaning, the whole of creation its center point and humankind its highest ideal.

The simple truth is this: We can trust life and accept ourselves because the invisible power in control of everything is friendly and has been revealed in Jesus Christ.

This is not the type of truth which we learn once and have at our disposal forever. It seems to fade from our minds, to get confused in various interpretations, to lose its effective power. Thus it is important that all Christian doctrines and practices continually point to and enliven this central truth.

The various Christian teachings are all organically related as various specifications of God's revelation in Jesus Christ. They exist, however, in a hierarchical order, which means that some are closer to the core message than others. For example, the doctrines of the Incarnation and the Trinity are at the very heart of Christianity while the teachings on the Assumption and purgatory are more peripheral. Our teaching and preaching will best serve a contemporary spirituality by respecting this hierarchy of truths. We must emphasize the essential dogmas while relating all doctrines to the core of the faith.

In striving to simplify our own understanding of Christianity, short creeds are a valuable tool. Creeds are an effort to sum up and point to God's revelation which always remains greater than any of our verbalizations. We need short summary statements of the faith which are adapted to the needs of various age groups and cultures.

For example, a short creed for little children might be:

Even if we do bad things
there is someone who always loves us
and we call him our God.

As adult, educated Westerners we might say:

The mystery
which is the source of our life
and the goal of our longings
is gracious,
has spoken through Jesus of Nazareth
and calls us to an abiding personal relationship.

In addressing people with a secularized outlook we can

state our faith simply: "Life can be trusted," or, "Constructive human effort is ultimately worthwhile." This can be specified by adding that the meaning of these assertions is most clearly manifested in the life of Jesus. Many such short creeds are needed and devising them is dependent on understanding both the people addressed and the core message of Christianity.

Working out a personal short creed which summarizes our own perceptions of Christianity is a valuable enterprise. If we can keep the essential point of Christianity before our minds and in our hearts, we are in a better position to manage the complexity which surrounds us.

Christianity then can be seen as the home of all truth, goodness and beauty. In moments of confusion and darkness we can draw upon the illumination provided by the life and teachings of Jesus. When our confidence is shaken, the abiding presence of the Spirit can provide a surprising strength. When complexity threatens our serenity, we can turn to the Gracious Mystery who continues to guide us.

Avoiding Trivialization

I meet a good number of people these days who speak about a thirst for deeper, richer, more satisfying, more integrating, more demanding experiences in their lives. If we use the adjective *religious* in a broad sense to indicate the mysterious depths of human existence, then we could call this phenomenon a "search for religious experience."

Many factors in our contemporary culture no doubt produce this spiritual thirst, including an expanding secularization, the dominance of technological thinking and insipid Church services. Here I want to concentrate on what I will call "the trivialization process."

Life forces certain routine tasks upon us which may seem trivial. It could be the monotony of housework, the drudgery of the factory or the boredom of the office. Our daily round includes waiting in lines and participating in superficial conversations. The very dullness of our ordinary routines can no doubt blind us to the presence of God in our daily lives.

It seems to me, however, that an even more subtle obstacle to achieving authentic religious experience is the trivialization of important human matters. Consider these questions: What happens to our sense of the tragic dimension of life when we read nothing but happy-ending novels? What effect do brief news reports which highlight the sensational have on our sense of the complexity of human affairs? What do long hours of passive TV watching do to our sense of creativity? Is our capacity for genuine emotional response affected by movies which portray superficial emotional reactions to real human tragedy? What effect do digest summaries of complicated ideas have on our interest in intellectual inquiry? When commercials link our deepest longings for love, a zestful life and freedom with cars, beer and cigarettes, what happens to our ability to appreciate the mysterious infinity of our genuine desires? An observation of the late economist E. F. Schumacher comes to mind: "If our ideas are mainly small, weak, superficial and incoherent, life will appear insipid, uninteresting, petty and chaotic."

From a theological perspective it appears that these powerful cultural influences help to diminish our religious sensibilities. The finite things of life become ends in themselves. Our sense of awe and wonder is blunted. The thrill of search and discovery is lost. The creative energies are diminished. Emotional responses remain superficial. The common element throughout is that some important aspect of human experience is rendered insignificant—matters of ultimate concern are obscured, complex issues are given simplistic solutions, vital human capacities are dormant. In short, the religious dimension of life is swallowed up by the "trivialization process."

What effect does this trivialization have on the human person? The German existentialist philosopher Martin Heidegger suggests a picture of the victim of this process in his descriptions of the "curious person" (cf. *Being and Time*, p. 214ff). Such individuals are not genuinely concerned with what life is all about, but are restless, always seeking the excitement of novelty. They are not concerned with knowing but only with having known. For them the pace of life is so rapid that there is no time to establish roots or really to enjoy the journey. They engage in idle talk and are interested in what "everyone" is seeing and doing. In relating to other individuals, curious persons quickly resort to stereotypes based on what "they" say.

Curiosity, as Heidegger sees it, involves a life that may seem exciting or "with it" but which, in reality, has no depth, no genuine commitment and no real authenticity. The curious person achieves a dehumanizing adjustment to a trivializing culture. The problem is so pervasive that we have to ask what elements of superficial curiosity exist in ourselves.

The search for religious experience often becomes part of the problem rather than the solution by being co-opted into the same trivializing tendency dominant in the culture. Cheap grace and easy answers abound. Popular religious books speak of quick and easy steps to spiritual enlightenment. Weekend gatherings are expected to produce sudden and long-lasting conversions. Difficult theological questions are covered in a six-week course. Many seek the joys of resurrection without following the difficult path of the cross. Emotional highs are sought without consideration of the dark night. Self-fulfillment is expected without self-denial.

If the search for religious experience is to overcome the superficialities of our culture, it must take a more serious turn. Superficial curiosity must give way to genuine concern. Idle talk must give way to deeper reflection. Following the crowd and "being in" must yield to action based on a personalized faith. The latest fad in spirituality must be seen in the light of the rich and diverse Christian tradition. Easy answers must be questioned in the light of the essentially mysterious character of our existence.

The fact is that diligent and intelligent effort is required to penetrate beneath the surface of our distracted and busy lives. We must go through the painful business of examining and correcting our spiritual blind spots. We must cultivate the habit of recollection and gradually attune our sensibilities to the presence of God. We have to find out what factors block our awareness of mystery and what remedies are needed to overcome these obstacles.

Most people find that results are related to systematic effort—a daily regimen, time for meditation, learning techniques of prayer, doing spiritual reading, getting sound advice. The temptation to quick results must be resisted. The spiritual masters spoke of dry periods, of the dark night of the soul and of the experience of the absence of God. It is not reasonable to think that people today are to be spared this struggle even though our culture is biased in favor of instant solutions.

Since it is precisely trivialization which helps to create the spiritual vacuum many experience, it should be clear that superificial activity, even of a religious nature, cannot fill the emptiness. Simply realizing this may help to free us to attack the problem more constructively through systematic, enduring and intelligent effort. Authentic religious awareness can be cultivated only gradually over a lifetime—with no illusions of perfect achievement while the journey continues. The Gracious Mystery reveals its full riches only to the tutored eye of faith, a disciplined self-awareness and a purified heart open to the Spirit.

Part Two
Concrete Experiences of the Mystery

This second part of the book focuses on various persons, events and encounters which have been, for me, clues to the presence of the Gracious Mystery. They are offered as a stimulus for your own reflection with the hope that they strike responsive chords.

Chapter Five
Wrestling With the Dark Forces

Work and Leisure: Finding a Balance

My spiritual director tells me I am a "workaholic." While I really don't believe that term fits me exactly, his observation has prompted personal reflection on the relationship between work and leisure. I have also been reading books on this topic and trying to learn from the people I counsel, noting the way their problems are similar to my own and pondering the advice I give them. A classic case comes to mind.

He was exactly on time, sharply dressed, obviously bright, socially adept; but beneath the surface lurked a curious disquiet. In response to my question, "Who are you?" he responded, "I am a corporate executive." He didn't say, "I am a father or a husband or a believer"; he identified himself with his job.

And he spoke truly, for he did perceive himself as almost totally constituted by his occupation. His sense of worth and dignity was tightly bound up with the socioeconomic status provided by his employment. He talked enthusiastically about what went on at the office and very little about his family. He was proud of his business accomplishments but seemed oblivious to questions of personal growth.

With prompting, he spoke about the other areas of his life. He did do some reading but most of it related to his business interests. He cared a great deal for his family but didn't have a lot of time to spend with them now. He usually brought work home with him which occupied him till it was time for bed. He figured his family understood; and if things ever slowed down at work, he would try to give more attention to them.

He did take a vacation with his wife to Europe for two weeks. He was sort of nervous and found it hard to relax, but they kept up a terrific pace and really got a lot accomplished. Of course, it had all been carefully planned ahead of time. They got through one museum—he couldn't recall the name—in less than two hours.

The importance of exercise had not escaped him. Racquetball was on his schedule two or three times a week, always played vigorously with a great competitive spirit. Those were his relaxing times.

But there was still that strange disquiet that had brought him to my office. He really wasn't very happy with his life. Something was missing. A vague dissatisfaction plagued him which he was unable to manage or even understand. He wasn't sure how his wife felt about many things, and their sex life wasn't all that great anymore. But, he surmised, that was probably just fatigue. He hated to seek help with all this, but the gnawing anxiety was just getting to be too much.

Where to start by way of response and advice? I honestly told him that if I had any good advice, it would be mostly theoretical and not the result of wisdom gained from lived experience. Perhaps, however, we could explore the matter together.

The kind of disquiet he described may well result from an imbalance in his life, from a preoccupation with work and a neglect of leisure, from an emphasis on efficiency and success to the detriment of spontaneity and enjoyment. The fact is that we are spiritual creatures who are immersed in a world of matter, a combination of freedom and necessity, a mix of soaring spirit and earthbound bodies. We need the unplanned and unpredictable as well as the planned and calculated. In a balanced life, there must be receptivity and surrendering as well as activity and conquering.

Some of our activity time should be aimless and spontaneous as well as goal-oriented and controlled. In short, we need a balance of leisure and work for a healthy existence. The problem for many of us, of course, is that the aimless, unproductive, passive, receptive, spontaneous, creative, leisurely side of life has been lost or diminished. The result is a truncated and perhaps vaguely dissatisfying existence.

Some efforts to redress this imbalance between work and leisure, however, can leave a person in the same disturbed condition. Some people, for example, who find their work draining or meaningless become compulsive and frenzied in their pursuit of leisure. A few hours of free time must be used productively; weekends involve a round of busy, exhausting activities; vacations are carefully planned and rigidly executed. Leisure time is then simply an extension of the attitudes and approaches which dominate the world of work.

Other people devote free time away from work to escapist activities: watching TV for hours with little conversation or family interaction; consuming enough alcohol to keep the mind fuzzy and anxiety at bay; daydreaming to block from mind the depressing prospect of returning to work. Leisure in these situations is simply a stultifying escape from the drudgery of work.

Healthier ways of dealing with the loss of leisure in our lives can be imagined, but they must be founded on a solid anthropology. Since we are truly enspirited bodies, the best of our human activities will include both a planned, purposeful, serious aspect as well as a spontaneous, aimless, playful dimension. In other words, when we are engaged in truly humanizing activity, there will be present both the effort to accomplish something and an intrinsic immersion in the activity for its own sake. When the former predominates, we call it work; when the latter comes to the fore, we name it leisure.

One way of overcoming this imbalance between work and leisure is by bringing more creativity, spontaneity and playfulness *into* our work. We can start with a steadfast refusal to make an idol out of our work, by identifying our whole being with our job or making success into an ultimate concern. Then we are free to search for ways to humanize our work. Assembly-line workers, for example, can humanize their jobs by betting on some variable in the material that comes down the line or by engaging in light banter with their coworkers. I myself once used the repetitive actions of my job in a coffee-roasting plant as a backdrop for a good deal of imaginative thinking.

Concrete Experiences

Service-oriented jobs provide an opportunity to enter into the personal stories of other people who often provide enlightenment and inspiration to those willing to listen. Homemakers can find a challenge to their creativity in trying to respond lovingly to the uniqueness of each of the members of the family. These examples remind us that we can all find ways of doing our work in a more leisurely or humane fashion.

Making an intelligent, systematic effort to bring more leisure activity into our lives is a second way of overcoming the imbalance which plagues many of us. We need to jar our ordinary assumptions about the primacy of work by recalling that important thinkers both ancient and modern consider leisure, not work, as the primary goal of human life. From their perspective work is for the sake of leisure and not vice versa as is commonly assumed. The truly human life is given over to philosophy and the arts.

This view demands that we begin to see the value of activities which possess no obvious purpose or payoff but which have a self-contained meaning. We can think of activities such as appreciating nature, discussing the great questions, meditating regularly, developing creativity, enjoying a hobby, playing wholeheartedly, moving slowly, reading poetry and fiction, praying wordlessly, being present to family and friends, vacationing restfully, contemplating beauty and finally, worshiping the Mystery. If we can convince ourselves that these activities have value, then maybe we will spend more time doing them.

Genuine leisure has nothing to do with stultifying escapism or frenzied activity. It demands that we find more time to activate our receptive and creative side. We must use available free time to renew our body, cultivate our mind and enrich our spirit. The attitudes developed can then flow back into our work so that it is less burdensome and more humanizing.

When the executive asked how he could start to move in this direction, I made some suggestions:

- Take off your watch when you go to Mass on Sunday.
- Read Josef Pieper's *Leisure, the Basis of Culture* or Sebastian de Grazia's *Of Time, Work and Leisure*.
- Read some poetry each day.

• Go to a museum and spend all the time with one or two paintings.
• Take a leisurely walk with family or friends.
• Go on a short retreat once a month.
• Play a sport solely for the enjoyment.
• Take the kids to a sandlot baseball game.
• Learn how to cook.
• Meditate regularly...

As I concluded my remarks the nagging question was still there. When will I start to heed the warning of my own spiritual director?

The Faces of Evil: Learning From Fiction Writers

THEOLOGIAN: I have called you fiction writers together because I think of you as the antennae of the culture. I am interested in the societal and personal demons which assail us today. From you, I hope to learn about the secret anxieties which afflict us as well as the texture of contemporary human suffering. In other words, *what face does evil present to us today?*

I am also interested in any wisdom you have for coping with these evils. My sense, however, is that you are more in touch with the problem of evil than with any genuine insights into dealing with it. Maybe the Lutheran theologian Paul Tillich was right and I should look to you simply to raise the questions and let the Christian tradition provide the answers. My Rahnerian training, however, tells me to be alert as well for any insights you might have into managing the human predicament.

Saul Bellow, let me start with you. I am impressed with your knowledge of the philosophical world as well as your ability to give voice to so many different types of people in our society.

BELLOW: Thank you. I do believe I have a feel for the alienation of ordinary people and the burden of guilt carried by so many. My mind is attuned to the sense of being imprisoned in a messy past, the feeling of isolation that most persons share and the terrible specter of death that haunts us all. To me, it is a question of whether we can carry on or not: *Can we, in meaningful fashion, beat the weight of our own ego with its accumulated guilt and mistakes?* This is why my characters are often overweight and feel sluggish.

But as you know from my novels—*Herzog* would be a good example—I am convinced that nihilism is misguided and that redemption is possible. I believe that a moment of insight can come when a person knows healing, sloughs off the burdens of the past and rediscovers meaning. Once I wrote that we are "not gods, nor beasts, but savages of a somewhat damaged but not extinguished nobility." It is that inextinguishable nobility that I like to stress in my fiction. It can be found when people break out of their own selfishness and manage to love another person.

But what gets in the way of this nobility is self-hatred, alienation induced by a sense of guilt and anxiety over death which can lead to eternal damnation. Sometimes we create impossible standards of conduct for ourselves and then feel all the worse when we cannot live up to them.

Do you remember when my hero Moses Herzog finally got over the guilt feelings connected with his failed marriage to Madeleine? The narrator put it this way: "It was a delicious joy to have her removed from his flesh like something that had stabbed his shoulders, his groin, made his arms and his neck lame and cumbersome." And then Moses writes a note to God: "How my mind has struggled to make coherent sense. I have not been too good at it. But have desired to do your unknowable will, taking it, and you, without symbols. Everything of intensest significance. Especially if divested of me."

That sort of sums it up: The guilt and self-hatred over failed relationships is cumbersome, but somehow it all has

significance if we can get our distorted ego out of the way.
Lately, I've begun to see the problem of human
suffering in broader societal and cultural terms. In my new
novel, *The Dean's December*, I have gained the confidence
to write about more public issues such as oppression in
Eastern Europe, the problems of the economically deprived
and the deterioration of our American cities. After all, the
job of the novelist is to raise moral questions and these are
the pressing problems of our time.

THEOLOGIAN: Joyce Carol Oates, perhaps you would like to
break into the discussion at this point since so much of your
fiction centers on the violence of our cities and the cultural
problems that affect us. Your novel *Them* gives a searing
portrayal of the anger, alienation and hopelessness which
existed in Detroit before the riots of the late 60's.

OATES: It should be obvious that violence is all around us. The
rationalists had it all wrong when they thought reason could
control the emotions. As a matter of fact, our passions keep
overcoming our reason. We seem bent on destroying
ourselves.

I think Saul is just catching up with the real
problem—*cultural* violence. I once wrote of our national
compulsion, a sort of demonic urge to use violence as the
answer to all problems. In my fiction I don't often make
judgments upon the individual involved in violent acts.
Rather, I simply lay out in detail the aggression that
threatens us all. If you are looking for some positive answers
from me, you may well be disappointed.

I do think imagination is crucial, however, and that we
have to impose form on the chaos. Perhaps this is the role
of the novelist and artist.

THEOLOGIAN: Dr. Allen, or may I call you Woody? I notice
that during this whole discussion you have been standing on
your head in the corner playing what looks like a clarinet.
Would you care to enter into the conversation at this point?

ALLEN: Yes, let us get down to the real existential problem of
evil. I'm talking morality and death, meaninglessness and
absurdity—you know, the large questions—like finding a

plumber on weekends. To me, the world is like one large concentration camp. The problem is that God is absent. I've been looking everywhere, in Manhattan and in people's interiors, and he just isn't leaving enough clues, no clear signs—you know, like a large deposit in a Swiss bank in my name.

If there is a God, and that is the only question that matters, then the most you can say about him is that he is an underachiever. I mean, like what has he really done about evil?

The question of meaning and death continues to haunt me, and I've tried everything to get rid of the ache in the pit of my stomach. The wild life with its hedonism is not the answer.

Some people think they see glimmers of hope and some answers in my latest movies like *Manhattan* in which trust in people and flashes of beauty offset the harsher aspects of life. When you get down to it, however, absurdity threatens us all. Yet I'd hate to commit suicide and then read in the papers that they found out God exists.

You have to excuse me now so I can get back to my Zen clarinet.

THEOLOGIAN: John Cheever, what do you think of all this heavy conversation?

CHEEVER: For me, the problem of human suffering comes in simpler and more mundane affairs: *People feel bored, locked into rigid patterns, suffocated in their own guilt.*

In my short stories the characters often feel confined by the banality of life and are struggling, in often restrained ways, for some measure of freedom. Remember the frustration of the guy in the checkout line at the A & P when someone jumped in front of him? That's the way the average person knows evil and the unfairness of life.

THEOLOGIAN: James Baldwin, you have been uncharacteristically silent.

BALDWIN: Well, you have neglected the real festering evil in our society—*the lingering problem of racism.* You whites are afraid of us blacks because we remind you of your sins, of your hypocrisy, of your willed innocence, of the bankrupt character of your white Churches. We blacks all know you whites, if you see what I mean. We had to learn in order to survive, but you can't stand to face us and learn the truth about yourselves.

Evil doesn't have anything to do with the Hollywood version of Satan but with the devil in you and me. The real problem is that we treat others as nonpersons and thus lose our own identity. That is genuine evil, and until we learn to love one another, we have no possibility of working out our true identities as human beings.

THEOLOGIAN: I am sure you writers don't like theologians putting your deeply felt perceptions of human suffering into tidy propositions. Yet I can't help but pull together for myself a profile of the cultural and personal demons you describe so well: the dark forces of death, absurdity, boredom, violence, banality and racism which threaten our cultural integrity and personal peace.

I believe, despite the power of these evil forces, our Christian faith offers us hope! It can be expressed quite simply: *The Mystery has revealed itself as gracious in the person of Jesus.* He did not, of course, explain the Mystery of evil but he did attack with extraordinary courage the demons you described. Perhaps on another occasion we could discuss the marvelous Gospel stories in which Jesus casts out the demons and cures the sick. We could also explore the meaning of the Cross as well as the empty tomb which symbolizes for us Christians the ultimate triumph over evil.

Dealing With Tragedy: The Challenger Disaster

I was sitting in a conference room at the University of Redlands in California about one and half hours east of Los Angeles. It was Tuesday, January 28, 1986, and we were enjoying a beautiful, clear sunny morning. World problems, parish concerns and morning angst had all melted away during my walk across campus as I gazed at the mountains in the distance. I was ready for some serious discussion with campus ministers from around the country, representing various denominations.

The local Baptist chaplain came into the room to lead a morning prayer service. He began by saying we were going to pray for the seven crew members of the space shuttle Challenger. The launch had gone badly; there had been an explosion; the crew was presumed dead. Silence, shock, and then the prayer.

My mind wandered. I had forgotten that there was even going to be a launch that day. It had been delayed so often. The whole thing had become routine. Once they got off the ground nothing serious ever went wrong. Images of the magnificent lift-offs from Cape Canaveral floated through my mind.

Then I remembered. The teacher was on board. She was going to teach some classes from space. As I began to think about the students the prayer ended. I had not prayed. After a few seconds of subdued conversation about the accident, the meeting began and the dynamics of the agenda took over. We were encased in our narrow world throughout the day, cut off from the media and all of the news reports.

After dinner three of us found a TV in the basement of one of the residence halls. As the narration and films appeared on the national news, the full impact of the tragedy began to hit me. Lift-off, marvelous as always, then the spreading fire, explosion, the sickening realization that nobody could survive, the disbelieving faces of loved ones and onlookers at the Cape, the spontaneous glee of the teacher's students turned cruelly to a confused sadness before our eyes. And all of it shown again and again so that we could not escape the harsh reality.

Then I was suddenly back in the sixth-grade classroom in Sandusky, Ohio, at St. Mary's school, teaching a religion class on the Exodus. Someone knocked on the door and said the president was shot. Some of the girls cried. I led a prayer, finished the lesson and headed for the TV to be joined with millions in a common effort to handle personal grief and national tragedy.

Now here we were again gathered around the TV trying to make sense out of a less momentous but very significant national tragedy. As we headed back to our meeting, I was glad no one spoke. Prayer came spontaneously as the faces of the students bombarded my consciousness.

Why is the shuttle accident producing such an intense emotional response from so many people, someone asked me the next day at lunch. After all, people are killed in accidents every day.

My initial response was that it had to do with the teacher. The presence of Christa McAuliffe made the mission special. Her personal qualities were so attractive: the infectious smile, vivacious personality, adventuresome spirit and obvious love for her family. Here was a committed teacher who took pride in her profession and cared for her students.

But she was more than an attractive, committed teacher. She came to represent all the dedicated teachers in the country and, by extension, all who take seriously the task of serving youth. Teachers, who labor with so few tangible rewards, were finally getting some recognition. Perhaps it even served to quiet the consciences of citizens who realize at some level that the general treatment of teachers is not only scandalous but detrimental to the common good.

At any rate, Christa McAuliffe was going to teach two lessons for students from space, raising her to the level of a national resource. This, of course, set up the special poignancy of young people around the country being brought into direct contact with a terrible tragedy.

Part of the intense response on the part of adults was a

desire to shield and protect these young people who had not yet developed the capacity to cope with tragedy. Perhaps some of us who experienced a loss of both innocence and optimism with the assassination of President Kennedy instinctively felt the danger to the young students.

While the role of Christa McAuliffe as teacher is crucial to understanding the national response, I have come to think that it is not sufficient to explain its scope and intensity. It now seems to me that the whole tragedy functions at the symbolic level. It points to the limitations of our most advanced technology. It destroys the implicit assumption that science is a quasi-religion which can usher in the new age. It reminds us that our scientific progress has a dark, destructive side as well.

The space program has held a privileged position in the American psyche. The astronauts not only had the right stuff but took on mythic proportions as people who could handle any problem with cool, rational detachment. NASA was one organization you could count on to get the job done. It was, quite remarkably, preserved from the criticisms leveled at most other institutions including Churches, universities, governments and the Peace Corps. The revelation that NASA is a human institution which has personnel problems and makes mistakes is greeted with shock and surprise—a clear indication that it had assumed a mythic quality in the national consciousness.

One of my former students, now working toward a doctorate in psychology, wrote me a very insightful analysis of his own reactions to the Challenger tragedy.

He began by noting the comment of a former astronaut who said that riding the shuttle was like being strapped to a bomb. Picking up on this image the student wrote: "Isn't Spaceship Earth also strapped to nuclear bombs?" The computer technology which could not prevent the shuttle disaster is the same technology which controls nuclear weapons. "If the shuttle can explode, anything including a nuclear war can happen," he concluded.

This is a perfect example of the way the Challenger tragedy functioned symbolically. It unleashed profound anxiety by exposing the almost unimaginably destructive side of the technology which many have assumed is our salvation and our best hope for a better world. Symbolic events touch individuals in different ways, but always with the potential to reveal depths ordinarily hidden.

One more utopian element in the American dream exploded with the Challenger. This tragedy joined presidential assassinations, Vietnam and Watergate in the attack on our national innocence. Afterward, some commentators returned to the theme of the importance and value of reaching for the stars. My instincts are to remain with the tragedy and to make sure we have absorbed its lessons before returning to such idealism.

The shuttle disaster tutors us in a proper respect for our creaturely finitude and our unavoidable limitations. It reminds us that science and technology, far from being salvific absolutes, are really ambivalent human achievements whose dark side must be squarely faced. The human adventure involves risk. Reaching for the stars sometimes brings instant tragedy. Each step on the journey brings us closer to death.

Such sober realism does not have to be morbid or paralyzing; it can free us to make the most of each moment. Hope is richer, deeper and more fruitful than optimism. Only when our field of vision is cleared of idols and naive utopian dreams can Christa McAuliffe reappear as a genuine symbol of the intrinsic value of the adventuresome spirit and of committed service. Realistic hope can only be grounded in the Gracious Mystery which energizes and rewards our always flawed and incomplete quest for the stars.

Struggling With the Fear of Death

Dear Louise,

I want to respond to your letter about your recurring struggles with the fear of death. The long sleepless nights sound horrible. Being stalked by terror is indeed a heavy cross.

Concrete Experiences

Your vivid description of entering into a dark tunnel with no way to get out touched me deeply. The recurring dream in which you wander through a maze leading to the top of a bridge where you meet a yawning abyss is obviously important. Since you wake up in a panic, I presume that it has something to do with the unknown and frightening aspect of death. I am reminded of your great fear of flying and the helpless feeling you experienced during the long illness of your sister before her death. It seems that the fear of death represents an ultimate inability to control life.

Your description of a formless terror with no obvious object brings to mind classic descriptions of anxiety. Many authors distinguish "fear," which has a particular object, from "anxiety" (*angst*), which has no clearly defined cause. It is simply terror over the threat of nothing, a deep fear of being totally dependent and ultimately prey to forces beyond our control.

It is almost as if your fears are bigger than death itself. I noted your comment that it would be easier to handle if you thought you were having a heart attack that very night. It seems that the unknown character of your terror is part of the problem.

I am glad that you are getting medication from the psychiatrist. There is little doubt that antidepressants work for some people. It does not surprise me that he is reluctant to talk about death since his training did not provide him with a framework for discerning its potentially deeper meaning. He might be of more help in sorting out your fears about making love with your husband. My sense is that it has to do with loss of control or committing yourself in a way which makes you vulnerable.

Louise, I can only imagine what these last few months have been like. As you well know, there are no easy answers, especially since this is a recurring problem. However, I want to offer you some thoughts on death which may be of some help to you in this terrible struggle.

Your tunnel imagery reminds me of the common elements in near-death experiences. These are the cases in which individuals have apparently died but are revived. In a typical portrayal a man, after hearing himself pronounced dead by his doctor, senses that he is moving very rapidly through a long tunnel. At the end of the tunnel, he glimpses spirits of deceased relatives and friends and encounters a being of light—a loving, warm spirit which nonverbally asks him a question which moves him to evaluate in a nonthreatening way his whole life. After this, he approaches a sort of boundary realizing that he must return to life on earth despite his great joy in being in this new world. When he is revived and later returns to his ordinary life, he is profoundly changed for the better and loses his fear of death.

Now I would not want to base belief in the afterlife on such experiences even though they are numerous and occur in various cultures. I suggest, however, you read *Life After Life* by Raymond Moody and reflect on the possibility that your terrifying tunnel might have a kindly light at the end of it.

Here is a suggestion on your maze dream: Before you go to sleep, imagine the dream in vivid detail and then suggest to yourself that as you step into the abyss you will fall into gracious hands which hold and protect you. There is a book by Patricia Garfield entitled *Creative Dreaming* which claims you can program your dreams in that way. I know some people who have succeeded with this method. You might have to experiment with various ways of giving yourself the positive suggestion before going to sleep. If it increases your anxiety, simply abandon this technique.

Your observation that you need a supportive community in dealing with this matter is right on target. I realize going to Mass makes you uncomfortable, but perhaps it is time to give it another try. Remember that all the individuals in the congregation are joined together in a common journey and have their individual crosses to bear. It would be ideal if you could find a few close friends in the parish with whom you could pray regularly and discuss mutual concerns.

You need to develop a more positive notion of death itself in order to gain some perspective on the dark side which currently dominates your thinking. The Russian existentialist Nikolai Berdyaev noted that life as we know it, if prolonged indefinitely, would indeed be hell because our deepest longings for a love imperishable would never be fulfilled. Death is our only chance to break out of the limitations of this world. It may lead to extinction, but it may also be a passageway into a richer, more satisfying existence.

Concrete Experiences

Karl Rahner sees death as the supreme act of our freedom in which we are called to hand over our very being to the Mystery which is the true goal of all our longings. Thus all of our life which involves self-surrender is a preparation for death.

With this in mind you should practice letting go of many things in your life. A good starting point is communicating more about your terror to your husband. He is such a trustworthy man; abandoning yourself more to your relationship with him will surely be helpful. You might find that being vulnerable and out of control is mysteriously and paradoxically liberating.

For us Christians, the key to the mystery of death is the resurrection of Jesus Christ. Try reading through all the post-resurrection appearance accounts in the Gospels. Select the ones which strike responsive chords in you, and meditate on one of them each day. Use your imagination to place yourself in the scene so you can feel the comforting presence of the risen Lord. Do not hesitate to express your terror to the Lord who experienced agony in the garden and abandonment on the cross. Then Jesus' trusting statements ("Not my will but yours be done" and "Father, into your hands I commend my spirit") can take on a greater significance and power.

The resurrection message is simple but supremely powerful: Life can be trusted; self-surrender leads to self-fulfillment; letting go means falling into gracious hands; death leads to life.

My prayer, Louise, is that in your moments of terror, this good news will be replayed in your head and resonate in your heart as a source of comfort and strength.

The Meaning of Resurrection

Perhaps we could call it "Easter and the Labyrinth" or, more dynamically, "Resurrection Contending With Chaos" or, more starkly, "Light Versus Darkness." However *it* is named, we all experience the continuing struggle to order and simplify our lives in a confused and complex world. Modern life enjoins upon us the task of keeping a proper focus in the midst of busyness, warding off the chaos which threatens us, maintaining perspective when confusion reigns, and preserving faith when things unravel.

The darkness named "complexity" is a powerful adversary in the quest for a tranquil spirit. A mother anguishes over how firm she should be with a recalcitrant teenage son. A father is in constant turmoil trying to balance his time properly between job and family. A corporate executive is totally confused by the ethical questions involved in key decisions he must make. A collegian is overwhelmed by conflicting pressures and wonders if it is worth it. A social worker wonders if she is really helping some of her clients on welfare. A professor is torn between the pressure to publish and her desire to be of real service to her students. A well-trained, intelligent young man searching for employment is completely discouraged because he cannot figure out how to break into the world of the employed. A minister wonders how he can stay afloat with the needs of so many people draining his energy and pulling him down.

As we reflect on these examples we are reminded of the power of complexity to confuse and overwhelm us. And we know again that deep, mysterious longing for peace and simplicity. Who or what will lead us out of the labyrinth and bring us to the place of tranquility?

The power of complexity is multiplied as personal concerns flow into societal issues. We long for peace and a secure future so that the human family can live in harmony. But how do we get there from here? What concrete policies are needed to ensure peace? What strategies will build up a consensus and eventually influence public officials? A woman in the peace movement says she is sick of all the political machinations but goes on to admit that she cannot withdraw from the struggle.

We long to feed people, to reduce poverty, to reach out to the starving children on our TV screens who are too weak to brush the flies away. People respond generously. Then we hear the food is delayed because it cannot be transported or it went to the army instead of those in need. A Harvard professor appears on TV suggesting the aid is doing more harm than good for some reason which is hard to understand. The mind reels and rejects this crazy notion. We must try to help.

We recall anniversaries of the ending of World War II and the Vietnam War. The struggle against Hitler appears clear, obvious, simple. Here was patent evil with immense power to inflict suffering and even to carry out an unspeakable genocide. For most, the course was clear. Such monstrous evil had to be fought with full force and defeated.

Recalling Vietnam evokes very different reactions. Passions still rage; clear-cut answers evade us. The concern for veterans with physical wounds and even deeper psychological ones is real and straightforward. There is a simple, pure empathy for those who mourn the dead and pine for the missing. But Vietnam brought ambiguity into the public consciousness. It forced many into questioning governmental policies. It ended a period of naive innocence for many citizens. Vietnam still speaks of confusion, chaos and complexity. Our national life can never be as simple and neat as it was before.

We recall as well the time when President Reagan visited Bittburg, bringing back the Holocaust memories. The liberation of the horribly demonic death camps, the pictures of the victims which have haunted our memories now for 40 years, Elie Wiesel pleading with the president not to visit the cemetery where SS soldiers are buried—all of this bombarded our consciousness. Here the darkness of complexity reaches cosmic proportions. We can discuss our personal struggles; we can debate the ambiguities of Vietnam; but we fall silent before the monstrous evil of the Holocaust. We dare not speak glib words about matters beyond our comprehension. The mind will not wrap around such an enormous tragedy. Simplistic explanations betray the vital effort to keep the memory of the Holocaust alive.

The harsh reality is that personal, societal and cosmic complexity threaten the simple peace for which we long. We can pretend ignorance, try to maintain a childish innocence, latch onto easy answers, or escape in numerous ways. The chaos of tragedy and the labyrinth of the everyday cannot, however, be forever banished from consciousness.

It is when such confusion and doubt invade our hearts that we can most profitably reflect on the meaning and power of the resurrection of Jesus Christ. The Church is wise in providing a long Easter season during which we can mine the riches of the resurrection. Easter Sunday can come and go so quickly. The hoped-for boost can be quickly dissipated. The very busyness of Holy Week and the ritual complexity of the ceremonies can obscure the simple message. We can get lost in faulty expectations and obscure symbols. Thus we can end up fighting complexity with limited and misunderstood resources.

We need time to ponder the meaning and absorb the inspiration of this great feast. The multifaceted significance of the resurrection can become clearer and more powerful as the liturgy puts before us, Sunday after Sunday, striking examples of the impact of the risen Christ: the forlorn disciples on the road to Emmaus recognizing the Lord in the breaking of the bread; doubting Thomas seeing wounds and becoming a believer; confused disciples eating with the risen Christ and gaining insight and courage. Thus we encounter individuals battling complexity and finding a renewed vision and strength. The season after Easter is filled with opportunities to drink in the meaning of the simple reality that God raised the man Jesus to life.

Time alone, of course, won't automatically unlock the depth of the meaning of the resurrection. We must penetrate to the core of this belief. We must be receptive to the action of the life-giving Spirit unleashed by the risen Lord. A simple faith—that is the key which unlocks the depths of the Easter victory!

What is this "simple faith"? The essential meaning of all the great Christian beliefs are illumined by the resurrection. The raising of Jesus to life tells us that the Mystery which we call "God" is not a capricious ogre or a harsh judge but rather a faithful friend. The God who did not abandon Jesus will never abandon us. The One Jesus called "Abba" always supports us and lovingly allures us into a better future. The simple truth is clear to the eyes of faith: God is absolutely trustworthy.

The resurrection teaches us that the darkness of death is not final or complete. The cross is not really a defeat but rather a healing victory. Death is revealed as a passageway to renewed life. The inevitable anxiety connected with death is surrounded by the conviction that we will share in the victory of the risen Christ. The simple if paradoxical truth is that death can be faced because it leads to a life-giving fulfillment.

The resurrection also instructs us in the significance and power of love. Love is the real energy which fuels the historical process. It is the binding force in relationships and the essence of our final fulfillment. In the death and resurrection of Jesus we see the generosity of love and the triumph of its power. The bonds of love are so strong that they cannot be broken even by death. The simple truth is that love is more powerful than all the dark forces including death.

The raising of Jesus revealed him to be the final prophet as he claimed. His cause was vindicated, his teachings validated. He is the absolute savior who has planted the seeds of the final victory. He is the life-giving Spirit who now transcends the barriers of time and space. In simple terms he is the Christ, the Son of the Living God.

The lucid simplicity of this resurrection faith arms us for the struggle against the chaos and confusion of an increasingly complex world. When our daily routine feels like a labyrinthian prison, a simple faith calls us back to the conviction that the faithful God will not abandon us. When the chaos of suffering and tragedy threatens us, a simple faith reminds us that the dark forces never have the final word. When we are tempted to paralysis by the complexity of our social problems, a simple faith insists that loving efforts on behalf of justice are never foolish or wasted. When we stand silent before monstrous evil, a simple faith reminds us that the risen Lord stands at our side—not with easy answers but with a sustaining power which can only be counted as a gift. An enlightened simple faith proclaims against all appearances that, in the struggle against the forces of chaos and confusion, the Gracious Mystery will ultimately prevail.

Chapter Six
Persons

Dorothy Day: Antidote to Escapism

Our recurring temptation to escape from the realities of life is not really surprising. It can be both frightening and fatiguing to tackle reality on its own terms day after day. A friend once told me that although he knew regular exercise would do him good, there was no sense in starting a program. He knew he could sustain it for a time, but the thought of disciplining himself day after day for an indefinite period was just too threatening even to begin. When we focus on the heavy and dark side of life, various forms of escape can become quite inviting.

Watching TV, for example, can be a substitute for serious family conversation. The stupor of drugs and alcohol can appear more inviting than honest self-criticism. Compulsive work seems to free one from the obligations of personal relationships. The rationality and civility of the academic world can shield individuals from facing the contradictions and entanglements of the rest of the world. The abstractions of theology can take the place of the genuine struggle for faith. A universal Christian love of all can be used to escape the obligation to love this needy person here and now. Vague hopes of improvement can substitute for constructive action. These examples are a reminder that we all have temptations to escape from the frightening aspects of reality.

In attempting to combat our particular brand of escapism,

Concrete Experiences

it helps to have concrete examples of individuals who have successfully immersed themselves in the messy reality of our contemporary world. It is precisely in this context that I find the life of the great exemplar of Christian charity, Dorothy Day, to be most significant. She is indeed a compelling and challenging model for a spirituality that is both engaged in the real world and energized by the gospel imperative to love individuals in need.

The facts of Dorothy Day's life are worth recalling. Born in 1897 in Brooklyn, Dorothy moved with her family to California when she was six and to Chicago when she was nine. She attended the University of Illinois for a couple of years where she wrote for campus publications but did not take classes very seriously. She went to New York in 1916; worked as a reporter for a socialist journal; got arrested for demonstrating for women's suffrage; started but didn't finish nurse's training; got married and spent a couple of years in Europe; wrote a novel which Hollywoood picked up; was divorced before entering a common-law marriage; and in 1927, gave birth to a daughter, Tamar. For motives that still seem mysterious, she had her daughter baptized a Catholic and then joined the Church herself—actions which painfully broke up the relationship with her unbelieving husband and estranged her from her radical socialist and Marxist friends.

In 1932, after a somewhat aimless period, Dorothy met Peter Maurin, a French peasant who traveled about, informally expounding the Church's social teaching in the context of a Christian version of personalism. She was captivated by his broad Christian vision which included concrete action on behalf of the poor.

On May 1, 1933, with Maurin's prodding, Dorothy published the first edition of *The Catholic Worker*, a monthly paper which she edited and contributed to for the rest of her life. The paper, which reached a circulation of over 100,000, provided a forum for an expression of the radical social demands of the gospel. Thus was spawned the extremely influential Catholic Worker Movement. The establishment of hospitality houses which fed, clothed and sheltered the poor in New York and more than 30 other cities helped spread the movement.

Through the years, Dorothy took active positions on a variety of social issues. She supported, for example, the right of

86

workers to unionize, including the United Farm Workers; fought
all forms of anti-Semitism; opposed Franco in the Spanish Civil
War (a very unpopular position with American Catholics);
supported child labor laws; fought social prejudices and
supported the civil rights movement; adopted a total pacifist
position during the Second World War; opposed Father
Coughlin's political views and anti-Semitic tendencies; supported
the Castro revolution in Cuba; and worked tirelessly for peace in
many ways including opposing the Vietnam War and protesting
civil defense practices in New York.

In great demand as a speaker and symbolic presence,
Dorothy traveled extensively, periodically visiting the various
Catholic Worker houses around the country, attending rallies and
demonstrations and lecturing at conferences. She traveled to
Rome twice during the Council, visited Cuba after the revolution,
went to Russia and England—always responding to some
concrete social need. Her last public appearance before a large
audience was in Philadelphia for the Eucharistic Congress in
1976, where she enunciated her usual themes of peace and love
of neighbor. After the talk she had a heart attack and spent her
remaining years, until her death on November 29, 1980, in
prayer and in close contact with her daughter and grandchildren.

What can we say about the spiritual development of
Dorothy Day? From an early age, she possessed an innate,
passionate concern for the poor combined with a vague sense of
mission to do something significant about it. She searched out
and gradually found appropriate objectifications for this passion.
For her, the bourgeois values of middle-class America were
superficial, and the socialist and Marxist approaches were too
narrow and materialistic. The Catholic tradition seemed to
include a care for the poor and provided stability and direction in
an aimless world. Peter Maurin presented a grand vision of a
concrete love that extended to the whole world. Her retreats in
the early 40's, under the direction of Father John Hugo, helped
to ground her notion of Christian love in a classical theological
tradition. The Catholic Worker Movement provided her with
scope and opportunity to work directly with the poor, to
contribute to the peace movement and to articulate her own
developing views.

In Dorothy Day passion fused with vision and intuition

with tradition to form the dynamic activist called by historian David O'Brien "the most significant, interesting, and influential person in the history of American Catholicism."

When we reflect again on the problem of escapism, the unique contribution of this outstanding woman becomes clearer: *She lived out and articulated for us a distinctive American spirituality* based on a concrete and realistic notion of Christian love. Dorothy read Dostoevsky's *Brothers Karamazov* in adolescence. Ever after she was taken by the monk Zossima's explanation of the nature of true love: "Love in action is a harsh and dreadful thing compared to love in dreams." *A Harsh and Dreadful Love* is the very fitting title of William Miller's biography of Dorothy Day and the phrase which captures the flavor of her understanding of Christian charity.

True love demands engagement with the needy, so Dorothy lived among the poor, patiently enduring smelly bodies and continual impositions on her time and space. Genuine love must not neglect those closest in favor of an abstract ideal, so she found time and energy for her daughter Tamar. Real love must be personalistic, respecting the dignity of the beloved, and thus she tried to treat the vagrants who came to her as unique individuals. Generous love sacrifices without return, and so she remained charitable to those who treated her badly. A constructive love tries to create a situation where the downtrodden can better their lot, so she fought for the right of working people to organize. A comprehensive love demands world peace and justice, so she protested all war. Christian love believes that Christ is to be found in those who suffer and are needy, and so she dedicated her life to helping them. Active love cannot be confined to words, and so she found herself in jail and on the picket lines, supporting the cause of justice and peace.

For Dorothy Day, love was indeed a harsh and dreadful thing. She knew her own moments of temptation to flee reality; but to a remarkable degree, she lived out her ideal of an active, involved charity toward individual human beings. Her spirituality reflects the practical, action-oriented, down-to-earth approaches valued by many in the United States. Her example can challenge our own tendencies to escapism and can provide a powerful impulse to find our own ways of *putting into action a Christian love which cannot avoid the harsh and dreadful moments.*

Thomas Merton:
A Fellow Searcher

Seventy-five people gathered recently for a weekend retreat to search for insight and inspiration from the life and writings of Thomas Merton. Many had a long-standing interest in Merton. Some recalled years ago reading Merton's autobiographical account of his conversion entitled *Seven Storey Mountain* which was on the best-seller lists in the late 1940's. A few had already read Michael Mott's clear, comprehensive and detailed biography with the fitting title *The Seven Mountains of Thomas Merton*. During the weekend there seemed to be a genuine fascination with the life and writings of this amazingly complex man. At the concluding liturgy, individuals shared favorite quotes from Merton and spoke of the impact he made on their lives.

This retreat experience raises some questions. Why would persons active in the everyday world of work and family expect to find guidance and encouragement from a man who lived most of his adult life as a contemplative monk in a Trappist monastery? What is the reason for the continuing interest in this compulsive writer who published some 50 books in his lifetime, left massive amounts of unpublished material and corresponded with over 1,800 individuals? Why have hundreds of books and articles about this man appeared each year since his tragic accidental death in 1968 in Bangkok while attending a conference on monasticism?

In his excellent study of Merton entitled *The Human Journey*, Anthony Padovano sees Merton as a symbol of the struggle of the 20th century. Just as Cardinal Newman summed up in his life and writings the spiritual quest of the 19th century, so Thomas Merton lived out and gave expression to many of the deeper problems of our own time.

Concrete Experiences

This is an intriguing thesis. From this perspective Merton appears as a man who asked the right questions and who struggled with the significant tensions built into the contemporary world. He fascinates us because we recognize ourselves in his effort to calm the restless heart. He challenges us because his amazing honesty and self-critical spirit call into question our self-righteous tendencies. He can help us because his key insights are gained from a genuine engagement with common human experience.

Merton is provocative because he uncompromisingly cuts through the superficialities and questionable assumptions of our culture. He is remembered, in part, because he wrote so well and gave us such striking images and poetic phrases. He is still current because he offered truly radical analyses of the enduring social problems such as racial prejudice and the nuclear threat. He is an inspiration because he continued to extend his experience and develop his thinking right up to his death at the age of 53. He is able to touch our hearts because he wrote out of a deep contemplative spirit which had plumbed the depths of mystical experience.

Thomas Merton clearly did not achieve total integration in his own life nor does he provide neat, logical answers to today's complex problems. He appeals because he is clearly a fellow searcher. He found a way to live well without having all the answers. For him the inevitable tensions of life were creative. He refused to accept easy answers just as he refused to abandon the search for an integrating synthesis. We go to Merton not for a panacea but for support in our quest and for the marvelous countercultural insights and images which dot his writings.

Merton struggled with the problems which still form the inner core of our spiritual quest. How can we maintain a prayerful attitude in the face of the demands of our busy lives? How can we find healing for the wounds inflicted by our personal relationships? How can we stay in touch with the rhythms of nature in a technological society? How can we reconcile our passion for freedom with the constraints of authority and tradition? How can we gain a healthy perspective on our competitive, success-oriented western culture? How can we best participate in the quest for justice and peace? These questions can be formulated in various ways and our struggles with them are colored by our situations and our personal histories. It is hard, however, to imagine an authentic Christian existence today which knows nothing of these problems.

Let us examine the way Merton handled the freedom versus authority problem in his own life. In his early years he suffered from a lack of consistent relationships with authority figures. His mother Ruth, who grew increasingly harsh and judgmental toward him, died when he was six. His father Owen, who was a wandering artist type, managed to keep his son with him for only brief periods of time and died when Thomas was 16.

Thomas lived in rebellious confrontation with his grandparents from age seven to nine and later described these years as desperate and despairing. Even before his father's death he began living in London with his godfather and guardian, Dr. Tom Bennett. Here he enjoyed the good life: money, entertainment, travel and the opportunity for a fine education. When Thomas failed to use his freedom responsibly, by doing mediocre academic work at Cambridge and fathering an illegitimate child, Dr. Bennett effectively ended his support. Merton then moved to New York and attended Columbia University where he combined significant academic work with a good deal of carousing.

After his conversion to Catholicism in 1938, his restless heart eventually brought him to Gethsemani, the Trappist monastery in Kentucky. In describing his entrance into the monastery in 1941 he wrote this revealing sentence: "So Brother Matthew locked the gate behind me and I was enclosed in the four walls of my new freedom."

Here we find a clue to his sense of freedom and authority. He was in danger of being enslaved by his own strong passions and his immense hunger for the fullness of life. He needed the rigidity of the monastery to control his appetites and to provide him with a circumscribed field within which he could labor effectively. The monastic life helped him maintain his sanity but it also constrained his freedom. He was constantly battling the authorities who wanted to curtail his writing and to censor his books. Roman authorities forbade him to write about war; his abbot long denied him his great desire to live in his own hermitage and made it extremely difficult for him to get permission to travel.

Concrete Experiences

Still Merton needed authority figures. This is especially clear in Michael Mott's very restrained account of Merton's relationship with a young student nurse which began during his recovery period in a Louisville hospital in 1966. By Merton's own accounts they fell in love and continued to meet and communicate for over a year. The relationship brought him great exhilaration but also great anxiety.

Eventually a conversation was overheard and he was reported to his long-time superior and sometimes adversary Abbot James Fox. The abbot placed an absolute prohibition on Merton's seeing the young woman any more. Though the restriction was not immediately kept, Merton wrote in his journal that "it is providential that everything has been blocked off at the moment. Perhaps it is saving me from a real wreck."

Deep down Merton sensed he was in danger of destroying himself. He needed Abbot Fox, who had so often angered him with his authoritarian practices, to help him channel his freedom. It is not clear how influential the abbot's intervention was in the eventual breakup of the relationship. It is clear, however, that Merton feared his own passions and instinctively sensed that authority was needed in order to establish control.

My impression from the weekend retreat is that the revelation of this relationship has enhanced rather than diminished Merton's status as a spiritual guide for many persons. He did indeed know the human predicament. The common experience of freedom as sometimes burdensome is reflected in his lifelong struggles. His mixture of rationalization and honest self-criticism strikes familiar chords. He alerts us once more to the dangers of a freedom which eclipses the light of reason. He reminds us that authority, structure and tradition are necessary components of a healthy life. His example moves us to discern which of our instincts we can trust and which are in danger of leading us along destructive paths. He challenges us to introduce into our own lives the precise disciplines we need to enhance and channel our freedom.

Thomas Merton speaks to us today not with the calm voice of assured answers but with the sometimes anxious but always hopeful voice of the searching believer. Precisely for this reason his words echo, affirm and inspire.

Martin Luther King: Drum Major for Justice

It was a simple, low-keyed memorial observance of the birthday of Dr. Martin Luther King, Jr. And yet, as we sang "We Shall Overcome" and listened to the familiar cadences and striking imagery of this master orator and homilist, I found myself deeply moved. The experience prompts reflection on the contemporary significance of this great man, especially in the light of the more recent developments of liberation theology.

1) *Martin Luther King helps us to see the world and hear the Christian message from the perspective of the dispossessed and the powerless.* While he himself grew up in middle-class economic conditions and enjoyed the advantages of higher education, he did experience striking instances of racial prejudice which enabled him to achieve genuine empathy for the oppressed. He gave voice to the unheard cries of the poor and helped put the cruel face of oppression on our TV screens. His preaching showed how biblical themes and images could actually be used as a catalyst for action on behalf of justice, rather than as an opiate to create passive dependency.

Those of us who enjoy status and privilege in our society can never fully appreciate what it means to be powerless and faceless; but the message of Dr. King with its powerful combination of insightful analysis and passionate concern can lead us closer to a sense of what the oppressed experience daily. His charismatic leadership of the nonviolent civil rights movement forced many of us for the first time to confront the injustice in our society. His example moved us to a greater empathy for the oppressed. He called for "nonviolent gadflies to create the kind of tension in society that will help men rise from the dark depths of prejudice to the majestic heights of understanding and brotherhood." He continues to be such a gadfly for us today.

2) *Dr. King well understood that the oppressors in any situation are always impoverished and distorted by their hardness of heart and moral blindness.* Prejudiced individuals use the oppressed class as a scapegoat on which they project their own hidden fears and unresolved conflicts. The dominant group rules out the experience of the outsiders, thus depriving themselves of a fuller sense of what authentic existence should be.

Given this insight King did not wish to defeat or to humiliate the oppressors. He wanted to liberate them as well from the enslavements generated by their privilege and their prejudices. He called for dialogue and cooperation in an effort to achieve a better society for all.

The Christian injunction to love enemies translated for him into a program for befriending the persecutors. His statement, "Hate is just as injurious to the hater as it is to the hated," is a timely reminder for all struggling for liberation today to channel their energies in constructive directions.

3) *King knew only too well that sin has been embedded in economic and social structures.* The family life of his people had been systematically destroyed by the institution of slavery. He had to sit in the back of the bus and could not eat at lunch counters because of laws and social customs which were unjust and dehumanizing. He fought against a political system which denied citizens their right to vote. He attacked the worldwide economic structure in which, for example, the destiny of Latin America is in the hands of United States corporations and the apartheid system in South Africa is supported by American capital and trade. He opposed the arms race between the superpowers because it threatens humanity with destruction and because it takes food out of the mouths of the poor.

In short, King had a deep and comprehensive sense of social sin and constantly worked for institutional change. He put it simply: "Compassion is more than flinging a coin to a beggar; it understands that an edifice which produces beggars needs restructuring." Thus he reminds us to be more attuned to institutional oppression of all kinds, and he challenges us to work for systemic justice.

4) *Dr. King spoke of the blindness of people who are imprisoned in their own ideology and selfishness.* They suffer

94

from a false consciousness which makes self-criticism impossible and obscures important truths. That is why sincere and dedicated people accepted the system of slavery and worked out rational, religious and scientific justifications for it. That is why there are good people today who simply take it for granted that citizens of the United States should be affluent while most people in the world are hungry.

Status and social location influence our perception of the truth. King's solution to this kind of moral and intellectual blindness was through the practice of love. To be in solidarity with the poor, to work for the liberation of the oppressed, to fight on the side of the victimized is to come to the truth in a new way. Loving activity brings new perspectives, reveals hidden contradictions and grounds the search for truth.

Liberation theologians say that *orthopraxis* leads to *orthodoxy*, which means that the concrete effort to liberate human beings and to build a community of love (orthopraxis) is the real basis for a deeper understanding of the true meaning of the Christian gospel (orthodoxy). Dr. King reminds us of this truth when he says, "We must love our enemies because only by loving them can we know God and experience the beauty of his holiness."

5) *He adopted a dialectical approach to his country and his Church.* This allowed him to criticize them vigorously and honestly for not living up to their ideals, but at the same time to draw on their resources and symbols in the struggle for human liberation.

In a spirit of patriotism he asked how we could tolerate 40 million poor people in our affluent country and why we had to think of ourselves as God's military agent on earth. In a spirit of loyalty he castigated the Christian Churches for their silence in the face of human suffering and for their tacit support of unjust social and economic systems. Nevertheless, he did not succumb to hatred of these institutions nor did he totally abandon them because of their failures. He called on them to be faithful to their true ideals. He demanded that America live out the true meaning of its creed that all people are created equal. He challenged the Churches to return to the sacrificial spirit of the early Christian community which enabled it to resist evil and to transform society.

Concrete Experiences

He wanted social change and he knew that this required the mobilization of the best of our common traditions. But the man who articulated the inspiring dream of all God's children living in peace and harmony also said, "To produce change, people must be organized to work together in units of power." Today's challenges continue to demand that we gather around shared interests and our traditional national and religious symbols in an effort to enlist as many as possible in the struggle to humanize our world.

Martin Luther King had a largeness of vision and a greatness of soul which can challenge the narrowness and pettiness of both those with power and those fighting for freedom. He exemplified in word and action the major themes enunciated by today's liberationists; but he always surrounded and supported his analyses and efforts by an emphasis on a nonviolent, forgiving active love.

"Love is the most durable power in the world," he declared with evident conviction. And in his role as a drum major for justice, Dr. Martin Luther King still summons us to follow his example of working for the liberation of all people through the power of love.

Chapter Seven
Life in the World

Athletics: An Encounter With Transcendence

True-believing sports fans really must initiate dialogue with the nonbelievers. The stakes are high—strained relationships, misunderstandings, even the breakup of marriages.

Some will say that we believers are fanatics incapable of dialogue and unappreciative of the views of others. We may be accused of being literal fundamentalists who think we have a monopoly on what is good, true and beautiful—or even gnostics who claim to have an esoteric knowledge which cannot be shared with others.

But true-believing sports fans have an obligation to say something of how we experience our world: the things that move and excite us, the way we are affected by heroes, the depth of feeling involved in being a participant or spectator. We should do this, not for the purpose of converting others or making them feel guilty because they don't share in this world, but to increase understanding and promote dialogue.

It is true that people have varying S.Q.'s (Sport Quotients); but a poor rating here does not indicate bad will or defective character. If we simply share our experience in an open way, then maybe others with lower S.Q.'s will be moved to tell us about similar experiences they have in other areas such as drama, music, ballet, politics, poetry or work.

Let me start by describing a memorable moment from the

Concrete Experiences

world of baseball: I am sitting watching a game between the
Kansas City Royals and the New York Yankees for the American
League Championship and the coveted right to play in the World
Series. Late innings in a close game. I am involved now—my
palms are sweaty, the excitement builds.

Physical memories of my own playing days come back,
stirring the bodily juices (the adrenaline is flowing, we say).
Psychological memories of watching and analyzing big games in
the past with my father are on the edge of my consciousness. The
whole thing is familiar—a comfortable, gracious world—yet at
the same time it is filled with the unique excitement of the
unknown outcome. I am a spectator, but somehow I am also
participating. Freed from emotional constraints, I am touched in
some mysterious way.

I turn to one of my colleagues who has recently come into
the room and announce to her that it is a crucial part of the game
and a classic moment is at hand: George Brett, the best hitter in
baseball during the season, is facing Goose Gossage, one of the
best relief pitchers in the game. Kansas City is two runs down
and has two men on base. I mention this to her because I like to
share my exceptionally keen insights into baseball and because I
want to alert her to the fact that I don't want to talk about parish
business or anything else right now. Fortunately, she has a fairly
high S.Q. and immediately comprehends the situation.

I am involved in the game—planning strategy, feeling the
pressure, watching intently this supreme moment of competition.
Gossage is throwing 97 miles an hour and his location has been
good. Brett is swinging better than anyone has since Ted
Williams hit over 400 back in 1941. He has studied carefully
under the guidance of the new guru of the science of hitting,
Charlie Lau, a mediocre hitter during his own career, but a
greatly respected batting coach now.

First pitch. Gossage throws his usual live fastball, but it
is a bit too good (too much in the center of the plate). Brett,
swinging with classic perfection, gets it on the sweet part of the
bat and lofts it into the right field seats for a game- and
series-winning three-run homer. A classic moment indeed!

In an after-the-game interview, Brett watched the film of
his home run. When he saw the swing, he uttered a spontaneous,
ecstatic gasp: "Oh my God!" The fruit of all his study and

practice—a picture-perfect swing with head steady, weight shifted forward, eyes on the ball, arms fully extended—was there operating in the most pressure-packed situation.

That brief moment of human perfection in a limited area called forth a spontaneous feeling for the divine. Brett then quickly, but more reflectively, added, "Thank you, Charlie Lau"—a recognition that he did not achieve this moment of excellence alone but owed much to his former batting coach.

The nonbeliever probably thinks these descriptions—and the enthusiastic reactions of sports fans in general—are overblown, out of proportion and inappropriate in a world filled with serious problems. I must grant that sports can get out of control, become an idol, crowd out genuine religion, function as an escape, promote destructive competition, and foster greed. It is true that some people mistakenly want to make athletics into a religion, an all-encompassing, all-absorbing way of life. Yet there is a way to participate wholeheartedly in the world of sports which avoids the temptation of idolatry.

Play, as all things human, is potentially revelatory. It can help attune us to the abiding presence of the Friendly Mystery. Sports, when they keep from being an ultimate concern, can enrich our self-experience and call our attention to particular characteristics of the divine/human relationship. Only the believers know this truth firsthand and from the inside, but it is possible to communicate something of the experience to others.

When I watched George Brett's home-run swing, a sense of excitement and appreciation took me over. Perhaps I was recalling all my own efforts to master the art of hitting a baseball: prolonged study of the theory, uncounted hours refining my swing, the pure fun of taking batting practice, the sweet feel of getting a base hit in the game—and the crushing realization that I lacked the physical skills to ever be a good hitter.

One part of my delight in sports combines an appreciation of the excellence of good performance with a sense of the discipline needed to achieve such skill. Joe DiMaggio was one of my first heroes and I thrilled to the graceful way he covered center field. One of the reasons I liked Al Kaline so much was the classic way he performed—poised and balanced at the plate, coordinated and confident in the field. I can find quiet delight in watching the shortstop on the opposing team go into the hole,

Concrete Experiences

backhand the ball, plant the right foot and make a strong throw to first.

The attractive point in all this is that the body is under control, a physical excellence is achieved, body and spirit are unified. Poetry in motion—we see spirit manifested in a responsive body. The knowledgeable fan applauds in appreciation.

We humans strive for excellence, long for a total integration, thirst for a wholeness that overcomes the splits and gaps that plague us. Mostly this drive is frustrated, but there are a few clues that fulfillment might be possible. The gracefulness of excellent performance in athletics provides such an intimation for the true believers.

Other activities, such as listening to good music, have a similar power. But for large numbers of people, the most involving, emotionally-charged experiences of excellence and integration are provided by the world of athletics.

Another lesson learned from sports has to do with self-discipline. It takes hard work to improve one's skills. Those who have participated in sports recall both the joy and the drudgery of practice sessions. Competition gradually compels participants to accept the reality of both skills and deficiencies.

For some, no doubt, coming to grips with the lack of athletic ability is traumatic and potentially harmful. Care and prudence are needed here. On the other hand, many have learned from sports valuable lessons about the harshness of life, coping with defeat, accepting personal and group limitations and the discipline needed for improvement in any area of life.

When I watched Brett's home run, all of these thoughts, of course, were not in my mind. I brought to it, however, a long personal history of playing and watching baseball, which helps account for my strong emotional reactions.

For true believers, sports are mysteriously involving, and religious language seems appropriate for describing the experience. There can be many reasons for this, including vicarious experience, hometown or school pride, the thrill of competition, the desire to win. But my experience tells me that one part of it is the combination of excellence and discipline which can point to the Mystery which both promises wholeness and demands effort.

Christian Commitment: Church and World

In a homily I once told a story of a woman who was experiencing guilt feelings over not being more involved in the life of her parish. She felt especially guilty because she had not joined a small group in the diocesan Renew program. When she came to me for advice, she said she was raising three children, which kept her mighty busy. She did visit a nursing home once a week to talk to some elderly people there, but she simply didn't have the energy or the motivation to get more involved in her parish, though she went to Mass there regularly. Some of her guilt feelings, she believed, were coming fom the hard sell she was getting from the parish staff and from some negative comments made by a few very involved parishioners.

As I told her story and commented on the extreme busyness and constant demands which constitute the daily lives of many people, I saw a flash of recognition on many faces in the congregation. The interest level seemed to pick up.

I went on to offer my opinion that her guilt, though no doubt very real to her, was misplaced and inappropriate because she was actually living out her Christian faith in a worldly spirituality that seemed entirely fitting for her. She didn't really need more involvement in her parish; what she needed from the parish was assistance and encouragement as she struggled to maintain her various commitments.

The response of people after Mass confirmed my intuition that this is a sticky question for many good religious people who attend Mass regularly but feel put off by the calls for greater involvement in parish life. One man told me he felt vaguely ill at ease around involved parishioners, and he thought my homily would help him deal with it. One woman said my comments helped her make a decision about dividing up her time. From her

Concrete Experiences

remarks I presumed she was being delivered from some guilt feelings as she opted for involvement in some secular rather than Church-related activity. This question of secular versus Church involvement deserves further discussion.

On the one hand, many people obviously hunger for genuine community, and parishes can meet this need. Some feel alone and estranged and long for a group where they will know solidarity and acceptance. Mothers who deal with youngsters all day want a chance to communicate on an adult level. Divorced people desire relationships which will revive their sense of belonging and acceptance. People who have moved into unfamiliar surroundings need a new network of friends and an environment where they will feel comfortable. Students away from home must find a new community which will call them to continued growth. Individuals suffering from depression and an unhealthy withdrawal into self need a larger grouping to draw them out of the prison of self-centeredness. People with great capacities for relationships need many communities to tap the multiple needs and gifts that constitute their psyche.

In all these situations, parishes can play a vital and necessary role as welcoming, nourishing communities. They can be places where diverse individuals can feel at home, can meet others who share their values and can overcome their narcissistic tendencies. A healthy local Church will provide a sense of rootedness and belonging as well as various opportunities to experiment with diverse types of parish involvement.

On the other hand, many people find this essential need for group solidarity fully satisfied in various communities outside the parish such as the family, the neighborhood, civic groups, professional organizations, political parties, service organizations and athletic teams. In fact, many people feel deluged with commitments, overextended in relationships, overwhelmed by the demands of the various communities to which they belong. They don't want another meeting to attend, or more drains on their time, or more friends to try to fit into their lives. Their heart desires peace and quiet, space to breathe, time for themselves and loved ones.

Those of us who are parish leaders must recognize that many good parishioners are not hungering for community but are satiated with relationships and commitments. Rather than being badgered into greater parish involvement, they need understanding and encouragement as they struggle to bring Christian principles to bear on the various communities which already consume so much of their time and energy.

By the same token, good but overextended parishioners should put into perspective the enthusiastic calls for greater involvement issued by zealous pastors or dedicated parish leaders. Their enthusiasm often flows from a genuine care for the parish and is not intended to produce guilt feelings. If parishioners learn to trust their own experience and to think for themselves in religious matters, they will relate in a healthier way to parish leaders.

What then is a parish to do for those good people who are constructively involved in the world with little time left over for Church activities? The simple answer is: *Support and encourage this secular involvement by providing a faith perspective and spiritual motivation.* Concretely, this means that parish leaders give parishioners a pat on the back for being good parents, hard workers and responsible citizens rather than a rebuke for not joining the liturgy committee or Renew group.

Busy people need to be reminded that Christian principles should govern daily life and that constructive activity in the world is a legitimate way of spreading the Kingdom. These people seek nourishment from the weekend liturgy precisely so that they can go back to family, job and world with the core message of Christianity more clearly in mind and the support of the spirit-filled community more deeply rooted in their hearts.

This focus on secular rather than Church involvement is not just an easy way out for people too lazy or self-centered to get involved in parish life. It is a legitimate approach to living the Christian life which is rooted in a solid theology. God can be discovered in the whole world and in the full range of human experience, not just in the Church or in explicitly religious activity. Jesus Christ spoke little of liturgy and official religious life and a great deal about everyday life and human relationships. The Church is not the Kingdom but a sacrament and instrument of the Kingdom of God. The New Testament (Matthew 25:31-46 is a good example) generally speaks about the life of charity and not Church activity as the criterion for achieving salvation. This does not mean that Church involvement is unnecessary or unimportant. Nor does it demean in any way the vital work of those who give so generously of their time and talent in direct service to the parish. It is a reminder, however, that the Church is not an end in itself and that it should not be made into an idol. Parish activity is for the sake of building up the Kingdom in the world and should not foster exclusivism or group narcissism.

The woman's guilt over not being involved in parish life is inappropriate because she is already truly cooperating with God in the struggle to humanize the world. She is already in tune with the Spirit revealed in the expectant faces of her children and the lined faces of the elderly she visits. She is living out a worldly spirituality which unavoidably teaches her something about patience in the face of failure and about the joy which comes from unselfish service.

This worldly spirituality, precisely because it centers so much on activity and involvement, forces one to look for doses of peace, refreshment and nourishment. The hope is that our parishes can provide this kind of spiritual help through vibrant liturgies which nourish mind and heart and educational programs which provide perspective and insight for activity in the world. With proper sensitivity parish leaders can provide these services without imposing guilt trips or suggesting that some people are second-class members of the parish! The key is to remember that those who practice a worldly spirituality make valuable contributions to spreading the Kingdom and manifesting the Mystery at work in everyday activity.

A Spiritual Program for the 'Modern Manager'

The man appears confident and assured, but I sense some underlying anxiety or disquiet. He has come explicitly seeking some sort of spiritual guidance.

Having worked hard all his life, he has risen to a high position in his corporation. He often takes work home with him. After cocktails and dinner he works for awhile and then usually falls asleep while watching TV. His wife complains about their lack of communication and his children are unhappy that he doesn't take more interest in their activities. Once quite active in his parish, he has dropped out of everything, though he still attends Mass regularly. He used to be very athletic but now takes very little exercise and has put on too much weight.

His problem now, he says, is this vague anxiety that he feels. Bored with work, he often feels uncomfortable in social settings, cannot sleep well at night and feels guilty over his family relationships. He has never sought counsel before and will not go to a psychiatrist. He is open, however, to any advice I have to offer.

This story reminds me of the cultural analysis offered by sociologist Robert Bellah in *Habits of the Heart*. Bellah describes a "utilitarian individualism" which characterizes our contemporary culture. It grows out of the Enlightenment ideal which celebrates both the autonomy of the individual over and against institutional authority and the triumph of reason over tradition. With roots in the social thought of Hobbes and Locke, this form of individualism sees society as an association of contracting individuals who all have their own distinct purposes and private goals. The rise of science and the industrial revolution feeds this trend by emphasizing the importance of economic self-interest.

One result of this individualism is the "modern manager type" who specializes in finding effective means to achieve economic success. He often does this without consideration of common ends, larger projects or even other more personal goals.

Such is the man seeking my advice. He suffers the consequences of living out the managerial ideal celebrated in our culture. This ideal lacks much that is truly human including personal growth, healthy relationships and a sense of sharing in a common effort to build up the community of justice and love.

With this cultural analysis in mind I made very concrete suggestions to the man. Together we worked out a daily regimen: work limited to eight hours; no work brought home; exercise each

day (we agreed on a half-hour workout during his lunchtime); 15
minutes a day for meditation (I taught him a mantra and
suggested he use it during his busy workday); at least seven hours
sleep a night; no napping after dinner.

We then went on to talk about his dissatisfaction with his
job. I gave him a copy of Richard Boles's *What Color Is Your
Parachute?* to get him thinking about the possibility of seeking
other employment.

He agreed that he would systematically build in time for
his family. He decided to take a walk with his wife every night
after dinner and to save Saturday for activities with his children.
Finally, I made a strong plea that he and his wife join their parish
social justice committee and work together on projects to help
those in need.

Those of us who counsel can always point to our failures.
In this case, the therapy proved to be quite successful and this
man is now living a much happier and more productive life.

What kind of theology stands behind this very directive
approach? We can begin with an analysis of human existence
which takes seriously the threat of sin. At the personal level we
recognize that human development is not an automatic process.
We are subject to concupiscence, which means that we are unable
to integrate all aspects of our personality into our fundamental
option for good. A program for spiritual growth which recognizes
the reality of sin will adopt a systematic program of
self-discipline to challenge the destructive tendencies which
accumulate in the human heart.

We are products not only of our free acts but also of the
society in which we live. Our social, economic and political
situations condition us. Evil becomes embedded in institutions.
We internalize cultural symbols and societal values which, in
turn, structure our imaginations and influence our behavior. False
consciousness is possible; we fail to notice the contradictions
built into society. The dominant group in the culture may not
understand the plight of those on the margins. Theology can be
co-opted by the culture to become excessively private and
individualistic. Since systemic evil or social sin is so powerful,
an effective spiritual program must raise consciousness and give
us a systematic way of criticizing our culture from the vantage
point of the gospel.

Finally, God's self-communication seeks visibility; the universal revelation given to all people strains toward explicit expression. We human beings need objectifications to express and stir up our deep relationship with the Gracious Mystery. We need reminders that grace is indeed more powerful than all sin. Our personal encounters with God's goodness are enriched by symbol, myth and ritual. Scripture, creed, dogma and liturgy point to the Merciful One and remind us of who we really are. Jesus Christ is the human face of the Father and the exemplar of full humanity. The "dangerous memory of Jesus," as Johann Metz reminds us, provides us with motive and means for unmasking the contradictions and injustices in our society. We need contact with the living Christ and with vital religious symbols in order to maintain energy and focus in the struggle against social sin.

In summary, a theological analysis of social sin and religious symbols reminds us of the power of institutional and social factors to influence our behavior. Those who have been taken over by the values of utilitarian individualism often need structured programs to free themselves from these cultural constraints and to open themselves to the liberating power of the gospel.

Ash Wednesday:
An Enduring Call to New Life

At campus centers and university parishes around the country large numbers of collegians still show up to receive ashes during Ash Wednesday services. How are we to account for the endurance of this traditional religious practice when so many other traditions have fallen by the wayside?

No doubt many more persons are aware that Ash Wednesday is coming than realize the feast of the Assumption, for example, is at hand. The much-publicized excesses of the Mardi Gras season call attention to the beginning of Lent. I should also add that informal discussions suggest that many collegians mistakenly think that Ash Wednesday is a holy day of obligation. Difficult as it is to understand this surprising interest in Ash Wednesday services, I think there is a good deal of genuine religious sentiment operative as these young people are signed with the ashes.

The ritual of ashes is tightly bound up with the essential death/resurrection theme of Christianity and with the fundamental call of the gospel to repent and turn our lives around. It is closer to the heart of Christian understanding and practice than many of the sacramentals which are largely ignored by young people. My impression is that many collegians do understand the signing with ashes as a symbolic call to spiritual growth and not merely a magical practice.

Concrete Experiences

Perhaps there is a residue of the primordial understanding of ashes as a sign of our mortality and consequent dependence on a higher power. Those appearing in sackcloth and ashes in previous times surely found it difficult to feel self-righteous. Collegians walking the campus today with a black smudge on their foreheads may be expressing their own sense of the gap between what they are and what they feel called to be—as well as making a statement about their Catholic identity.

Whatever the reason for Ash Wednesday's appeal, the liturgy does challenge all of us to refocus and reinterpret the essential meaning of this traditional symbolic action. It is obviously a call to repentence, an invitation to enter wholeheartedly into the Lenten season, an opportunity to think seriously about needed discipline and a summons to more committed discipleship.

Sometimes this call has been given a heavy, moralistic tone. "Dust you are and unto dust you shall return" spoke to some individuals of essential depravity, of abiding unworthiness, of the threat of damnation. For those fighting to overcome a poor self-image and low self-esteem, this message could become one more obstacle to genuine growth.

Even for the more healthy-minded, this traditional call to repentance sometimes appears as part of a destructive religious strategy more interested in fighting pride than building up self-confidence. The wisdom of this strategy is very questionable given the tremendous fragility of the ego structure of most persons. Think of how simple statements of criticism or acts of rejection can shake our confidence and produce self-doubt. Consider the human hunger for affirmation. Ash Wednesday services which play to guilt feelings and promote a sense of inferiority distort the overall meaning of this symbolic action.

On the other hand, "Repent and believe the Good News" suggests a larger context for understanding our traditional practices of mortification, asceticism and self-denial. This phrase, said as our foreheads are signed with ashes, reminds us of Lent's positive thrust: Penance has to do with the gospel message that we are encompassed by God's saving love. We are engaging in self-discipline in order to become more receptive to the Lord's healing touch. We give things up in order to open up a space that can be filled with the life-giving Spirit. Mortification is for the sake of growth. We are not engaged in a masochistic program of self-deprecation but a positive effort to move toward a healthier Christian maturity.

This larger context for viewing Lenten repentance suggests a general strategy for choosing our Lenten penances. First, we begin with an assessment of what kind of person we want to become, or what virtues we wish to cultivate in order to become our better selves. Then we try to discern the precise obstacles to this particular development. Finally, we choose a penance which is designed to overcome or liberate us from the obstacles.

A shy person who wants to be more outgoing, for example, might decide to speak openly with one other individual each day. A person who wants to be liberated from a suspected drinking problem might try to drink moderately during Lent as a test to see if this is possible. An individual who wants to overcome egocentrism might try to pay someone an honest compliment each day. A person who would like to be more easygoing might decide to meditate 15 minutes a day. Someone hoping to increase daily energy level might take on a program of regular exercise and balanced diet. An individual who wants to get more out of the liturgy might try reading the Scripture passages ahead of time.

Sometimes the penance chosen according to this strategy might seem strange from a traditional viewpoint. In one Ash Wednesday homily I mentioned that my spiritual director felt that I had not achieved a proper balance between work and leisure and that, therefore, a good Lenten penance for me would be to go to more movies, plays and parties. With this same approach in mind, we can imagine some unusual penances being chosen: getting more sleep, reading more novels, making love more often, speaking more about one's own accomplishments, eating more food. The point is this: A Lenten penance should be chosen to overcome obstacles to a fuller response to the promptings of the Spirit.

One of the refreshing aspects of the Lenten liturgies is the reading of the Transfiguration story on the second Sunday. It provides the reader with a glimpse of the true but usually hidden nature of Jesus and serves as a foreshadowing of his resurrection. Placed in the midst of the Lenten season, it reminds us of the victorious character of Christianity, offers encouragement for the long haul and provides a positive perspective for viewing penitential practices.

We do penance not to tear ourselves down but to open ourselves up for Spirit-inspired growth. We struggle with discipline not because we hate ourselves but because we love the Lord. We choose penitential practices not to conform to a traditional piety but to deal constructively with our unique gifts and limitations. We give good things up not to inflict pain but to liberate ourselves from compulsions. We receive the mark of the ashes not as a superstitious practice but as a powerful symbol of our desire to be more open to the transfiguring Mystery which calls us to greater growth.

Advent: Learning How to Wait

Advent is the time in which we await the coming of the Lord. The rich symbolism of this liturgical season evokes a sense of longing and anticipation as we wait for the celebration of Christmas. Advent strikes responsive chords with so many who are serious about the spiritual life because it expresses in ritual, symbol and story our ordinary experiences of expectation, anticipation and hope. We all know the struggle to give meaning to the waiting which is part of our lives.

We grow up having to wait. "When you get older you can go to school." "Wait until next year and you can get a car." "Study hard because before long you will be going off to college." "Wait until you graduate and then you can get a job and make your contribution." "Why don't you wait a little longer before you get married?"

Waiting remains an essential element in our everyday life. We wait for the phone to ring, for the work week to end, for vacation to come, for the paper to arrive and for the sun to appear. Sometimes waiting takes on greater urgency. When will the pain let up? How soon will he face his alcoholism? Is the marriage about to end in divorce? How long does she have to live? Will we achieve peace or do we await nuclear destruction?

Further reflection on waiting reveals other questions which arise from the very core of our being. Will the deepest longings of our heart for a love imperishable and for a meaning beyond doubt be forever frustrated? Are we waiting in vain? Is there any sense to staying on alert? Are all the delays simply signals that we will never arrive? Are we finally doomed to frustration like the characters in Samuel Beckett's *Waiting for Godot*? Waiting is indeed tied up with our dependency as creatures. It can lead us to question the very existence of a final destination since the goal always seems to exceed our grasp.

There are various ways to handle the waiting we experience in life. Some of these are unhealthy and finally destructive. We can live with continual frustration, impatient with delays and excessively irritated by uncertainty. Waiting in line can raise blood pressure. Anxiety over how a relationship will turn out can lead to compulsive behavior. At the other extreme, waiting can become a passive dependency in which a person simply drifts along, a victim of the fates. Waiting for the perfect job can lead to inactivity. Anxiety over an unknown future can lead to paralysis. Relationships can flounder in mediocrity because we are too fearful to act to improve them. Passivity can become a way of life.

The Church's liturgy, like all good ritual and symbol, helps us to understand and order the depth dimension of our lives.

Advent instructs us in healthy waiting and proper anticipation. This season has the paradoxical power both to quiet our hearts and sharpen our expectations. The great Advent figures of John the Baptist and Mary of Nazareth are present as flesh-and-blood models who can teach us how to wait with a healthy anticipation for the coming of the Lord. The Baptist, blessed with a clear sense of his role as forerunner and herald, is nevertheless not lulled into passivity waiting for the coming of the great and powerful one. Rather, he goes into the desert and preaches the baptism of repentance. He instructs tax collectors and soldiers in their proper obligations. Lay leaders, the entrenched collaborators and the puppet king are all targets of his searing criticism. He is actively engaged in the task of clearing a straight path and making the rough ways smooth so that the people can recognize the salvation of God.

For all this courageous activity, the Baptist ends up constrained in prison, forced to wait, deprived of the contact with Jesus which fueled his dreams. The lonely waiting takes its toll and he begins to waver and to doubt. Is Jesus the one we have been waiting for, or must we wait still longer for another? The answer comes back: The sick are cured and the poor hear the Good News. There is no need to wait for another. The long hours of confinement continue, but we can imagine John awaiting his fate with a renewed sense of inner peace because the Lord has come indeed.

Mary, the maid of Nazareth engaged to Joseph, appears in the Scriptures as one awaiting a word. On alert, she hears the message of her favored status and her crucial role. Not content with passive acceptance, she questions the very possibility that she could be the mother of the long-awaited messiah. Satisfied with the response, she opens herself completely to God. Thus she becomes totally receptive and the wondrous deed is accomplished. The ever-present Mystery becomes personally, definitively and irrevocably present in our history. The Word becomes flesh. Human existence realizes its full potential. Responsive waiting issues in the fullness of life. Then the extraordinary yields to the ordinary. Mary springs into action and goes with haste to visit and assist her pregnant kinswoman, Elizabeth.

In the stories of John and Mary, Advent and Christmas are revealed as essentially related. History has prepared for the Incarnation. A proper receptivity enables us to recognize the presence of the Mystery. Healthy activity prepares for the coming of the Lord. The dynamic synthesis of waiting and acting, of receptivity and effort proves to be fruitful and blessed by God.

From this perspective our waiting can never be the same. The message of Advent and Christmas challenges our impatience and lethargy and heals our frustration and anxiety. We are called to wait with greater calmness, to act with greater resolve and to live with greater hope. Thus we wait not as bewildered voyagers seeking a distant port, but as members of a family already comforted by the presence of our elder brother. Rather than speaking of a "second coming" or "the return of the Lord," we should speak about the Risen Christ who is already present and who calls on us to cooperate in completing his work.

Christmas completes Advent by reminding us that waiting is not in vain. The celebration of the Incarnation will have greater power and meaning if we prepare well by managing our days with faith and intelligence and by cultivating a prayerful and receptive spirit. Then we can pray with understanding and conviction: "Come, Lord Jesus, transform all our waiting so that the light of Christmas can shine ever brighter."

Advent: A Two-Track Approach

"This year I'm going to get into Advent and prepare for Christmas in a truly spiritual way."

"All the consumerism is not going to upset my value system nor all the busyness destroy my peace of mind."

"This season is going to be a time of spiritual growth, and when Christmas comes it will find me prepared to celebrate the coming of the Lord in a special way."

"I want Advent to be a religious season for my family so that the kids have an appreciation of its deeper meaning."

"The liturgy is so beautiful during this season and my plan is to meditate on the Sunday readings for about 10 minutes each day."

"We are going to cut down on gift-giving this year and emphasize the real meaning of Christmas."

These resolutions to take Advent seriously and to Christianize the Christmas season sound very familiar. They represent the good intentions of many committed Christians. Some dedicated individuals and good families are successful in creating a prayerful, expectant outlook during the preparation for Christmas despite the demands of the season.

Many other sincere Christians, however, find that, despite repeated efforts, they cannot overcome or transform the consumerism, materialism and busyness of the Christmas season. Good resolutions are overwhelmed by the demands of preparing for the secular celebration of Christmas. Attempts to integrate the Advent symbols with busy December days just do not work. The effort to cultivate a patient, quiet attitude encounters more confusion and noise than usual. The figure of Santa Claus tends to push the Son of David to the margins while obscuring completely the great Advent figures of John the Baptist and Mary of Nazareth.

For the people who have struggled but failed to get Advent ordered according to Christian values, the call to Christianize the secular celebration of Christmas may produce more guilt than enlightenment and inspiration. *Part of the disquiet many experience at Christmas comes from failed ideals, broken resolutions and unresolved conflicts between secular and religious values.*

What, then, is the role of Advent? How can Christmastime be celebrated by sincere Christians who have, year after year, failed to overcome the dominant secular mood of the season?

I propose a two-track approach: On one level we consciously and calmly accept the reality of the secular celebration of Christmas; at the same time we cultivate a separate, liturgically-based preparation for the coming of the Lord in our hearts.

The key to this approach is giving up the attempt to Christianize the secularized version of the Christmas season in an *explicit* way. Instead, we Christianize it *implicitly* by accepting it on its own terms and finding the Lord in both its joys and its burdens. This acceptance can free us to develop in a peaceful, if limited, way the second track which flows from the beautiful Advent liturgy toward a deeper awareness of the presence of the Lord. Let me try to explain what I have in mind.

The first track is a familiar one to all of us. It begins with the advertising hype weeks before Thanksgiving and culminates in the sharing of gifts on Christmas. It includes, on the one hand, an intriguing mix of marvelous parades, thoughtful gift selection, enjoyable parties, comforting family gatherings, smiling children, jovial Santa Clauses and genuine giving. On the other hand, there are the frayed nerves, crowded stores, tiring preparations, excessive partying, phony advertising, demanding children, abrasive family relationships and routine giving.

Most of this has no clear connection with the explicit celebration of the coming of Jesus Christ and is indeed directly opposed to the prayerfully attentive attitude suggested in the Advent liturgy. If accepted on its own terms, however, this track provides a lot of fun and a chance to renew relationships. The season can teach us the joy of giving as well as the importance of learning patience, recognizing our limitations and cultivating our reflective life. The Spirit of Christ can surely be found in these intensified joys and burdens without pretending that they are an authentic expression of Advent themes or a consistent way of preparing for a religious celebration of the Incarnation.

The second track begins with the first Sunday of Advent, moves quietly through a month of liturgically-based reflection and culminates in an increased awareness of the continuing and definitive presence of the risen Lord. It includes purple vestments, readings from the prophets, moments of silence, messages of hope, imaginative talk of the end-time, beautiful stories of Mary and the Baptist, and challenges to remain alert. This has everything to do with a proper preparation for an explicitly religious celebration of Christmas and with a heightened awareness of the coming of the Lord.

The reflective mood and large perspective of this second track stand in sharp contrast to the noisy busyness and limited viewpoint of the first track. We need to cultivate this religious approach so that it runs deeper and wider than the secular route to Christmas. Our strength will come from the weekend liturgies and the few seconds of silence snatched from the daily clamor.

I envision carrying the Advent message into Christmas day like a treasure held quietly in mind and heart. There it can enrich our celebration of the Mass and flow into the rest of the day encompassing the limitations of gift-giving and filling the emptiness which often accompanies the materialism of the season.

Some will object to such an apparently limited and even schizophrenic approach. I would certainly admit that some people can make more out of Advent and should. But I would also insist that an authentic spirituality must be realistic and not lead to inevitable frustration and guilt. Attempting to Christianize

Concrete Experiences

the Christmas season by changing cultural patterns simply
doesn't work for many of us. We are better off enjoying without
guilt the secular path to Christmas while preserving the Advent
message in our heart. Thus, with less dissonance and a greater
sense of integration we can move toward a proper celebration of
the Incarnation. Reflection on the Mystery drawn near and
abiding forever in the person of Jesus the Christ moves us to
prayer:

O God, great beyond words and images,
Source of Activity and Goal of Silence,
we offer Advent prayer and Christmas celebration to you.
Out of the noise and busyness
we cry out for moments of silence and rest.
Teach us to fill in the valley of self-loathing
and to level the mountains of self-sufficiency
in order to smooth the way for your coming.
Let the discipline of the Baptist
and the responsiveness of Mary
touch our hearts and shape our conduct.
May the hidden truth of mystery-bound graciousness
spring forth in the midst of struggles for silence.
We would be on alert, Father,
for the secret comings of the Wonder-Counselor
and Prince of Peace.
When the Word leaps down from the heavens
and rises up from the depths of the daily round,
let it be light for our darkness.
O God of maternal care,
make us renewed tellers of your tale of Love made flesh
and enlightened bearers of your message of Peace on earth.
This Christmas we pray
that our loved ones and friends know our care
and that the liturgy be bright
with angelic hymns of glory and praise.
May our family gatherings be filled with peace and harmony,
and our gift-giving move beyond the emptiness of routine
toward the fullness of the Spirit.
And, Father-Forever,
let the reign of justice expand,

118

as we extend our celebration of the birth of the God-Hero,
into tomorrows filled with challenge and hope
for the completion of his work.
Amen.

Christmas: Celebrating the Word Made Flesh

The doctrine of the Incarnation celebrated at Christmas proclaims
that the all-powerful God does not remain remote and abstract.
Christmas is a dramatic reminder that the all-powerful God is
personally present in our history and experience. Sentimental and
superficial celebrations of Christmas, however, can obscure this
vital connection between the Incarnation and our daily struggles.
The infancy account in the Gospel according to Matthew is a
great corrective to this tendency to divorce the birth of the Savior
from real life concerns.

Let us allow our imaginations to roam as we consider the
hero of Matthew's powerful and moving story. Joseph is first
introduced as the son of Jacob in a long lineage going back
through King David to the patriarch Abraham. Life looks
promising for Joseph.

Secure in his job as a carpenter in the small town of
Nazareth, he has recently been officially betrothed to an
especially virtuous 12-year-old girl by the name of Mary. We
imagine him happily preparing for a joyous consummation of his
marriage when he will take Mary to his home according to the
customs of his people.

And suddenly the bottom drops out. The unthinkable
has happened. Mary is pregnant and Joseph is not the father.
Her evident infidelity cuts into his heart. Engulfed with the
frustration of a failed dream, he struggles to determine his course
of action.

Concrete Experiences

The Jewish Law which has shaped his consciousness and molded his character calls for divorce; and so it must be. He cannot, however, bring himself to inflict on her the full rigor of the Law which calls for stoning or the custom of public denunciation. He will divorce her quietly and not subject her to a public trial. The decision is one of conscience and compassion, but it brings little peace and much pain.

Before he can act on his intention, Joseph has a very mysterious dream. An angel of the Lord appears in the dream telling him to complete the marriage by taking Mary to his home. It is by the power of a spirit which is holy that she has conceived this child. She will give birth to a son and Joseph will have the honor of naming the child. He will be called "Jesus" because he will save his people from their sins.

When Joseph awakes from his dream, it all seems too good to be true. Mary is vindicated. They can complete their marriage. His dashed hopes spring back to life. But can the dream be trusted? Is the meaning clear?

Joseph believes that Yahweh speaks to individuals through dreams. After all, he is named after the patriarch Joseph, the great interpreter of dreams. The decision is swift; faith prevails. Joseph takes Mary into his home.

The pain of those days of doubt and anguish remain as a permanent part of his memory. But in the moments of bliss with Mary at his side he realizes anew that in the darkest moments Yahweh has been near.

The trip to Bethlehem is difficult; but the birth is marvelous. Joseph accepts the boy as his own, naming him Jesus. The visit of the astrologers from the East brings its own special joy. Joseph loves to show off his son and appreciates all the attention directed towards Jesus.

An ominous shadow, however, quickly falls over the whole occasion. The astrologers report their own dream clearly instructing them not to report back to Herod but to return to their own country by a different route. Joseph, realizing that Herod is a cruel tyrant, fears his mad and unpredictable behavior.

Joseph's worst fears are realized when the next night the angel of the Lord appears in a dream instructing him to flee with Mary and Jesus to Egypt. Herod is searching for Jesus in order to kill him. There is no hesitation or doubt. The message of the dream is clear. The forces of evil are poised to strike his own son. It is like a great struggle between good and evil. They will leave that very night for Egypt as the angel has commanded.

During the journey, Joseph thinks of his namesake Joseph and the patriarch Jacob, both of whom had made their own journeys to Egypt centuries before. He recalls the story of Moses and the way he was saved in Egypt from the hands of a wicked king. Perhaps there is some deeper meaning in this whole tragic event.

When Joseph hears that Herod has slaughtered so many innocent children in his twisted effort to wipe out any potential rivals, he is filled with a strange combination of anger and guilt. He and his family are safe; others have paid the price. Why does Yahweh allow such monstrous evil? How can the human heart become so perverted? The Sacred Books offer him comfort but few answers.

While in Egypt Joseph longs for the chance to return to his homeland. The family is close, but living as aliens is not easy. Finally the good news comes by way of another dream: They can return to Israel because Herod is dead. Joseph, who has learned to trust his dreams, wastes no time in beginning the journey home. As they travel, he talks with Mary about the history of their people. They are repeating the Exodus led by Moses centuries ago. Yahweh is saving his people again. Their son Jesus, who seems to have such a special mission, is being called out of Egypt just as was Israel of old.

As the family gets closer to their homeland, Joseph hears that Herod's son Archelaus has succeeded his father as king of Judea. He is a cruel dictator and rumor has it that he ushered in his reign with a massacre of three thousand people. Joseph, fearing the worst, wonders what he should do. Pondering all they have been through, he feels good about the way he has responded to the messages in his dreams. He has been able to marry the woman he loves. He is proud of his son and has great hopes for him. Functioning as a good father should, he has protected his family in very difficult circumstances. Is it now all to end in tragedy? Will he fail to find a home for his wife and son? Will they fall victim to another deranged tyrant?

One night after his mind has been working overtime on these questions, the answer comes once more in a dream. This time Joseph does not recall an angel in his dream but the message is still clear. He should go to Galilee in the north where Herod Antipas is ruling. He and his family should settle in Nazareth.

As the family heads for Nazareth, Mary reminds Joseph that their son will be called a Nazorean, which will indicate both his hometown and his calling as a Nazarite—one dedicated to God's service from birth. Joseph smiles at the clever play on words. He has always loved Mary's quick wit. It is strange the way he feels more confident in her presence. In these moments it is clear to him that Yahweh is indeed a faithful God. And when they join together gazing upon the face of their son Jesus, they see a continuing reminder that, despite personal struggles and societal evil, Yahweh never abandons his people.

Matthew's imaginative infancy account woven together out of a sequence of dreams, Israelite history and enigmatic Scripture quotes frees us to do some imagining of our own. His beautiful story is a "Gospel in miniature," a portrayal of the Good News that God is near and bringing ultimate victory over evil. Matthew speaks to us of the realities of the struggles we all know. His hero Joseph can be seen as a man not only of upright character, but of strong emotion as well.

Recalling the human struggles suggested by Matthew's familiar story is a good way to prepare for a more realistic and rewarding celebration of the Word becoming flesh.

Christmas: A Celebration for Adults

We need to find ways of celebrating Christmas in a more adult fashion. The way it is now, we seem to celebrate mostly through the children. While that provides much joy and genuine religious experience, it is not enough to meet our emotional and intellectual needs. Nor does it match the full meaning of the great mystery of the Incarnation.

Youngsters clearly dominate the Christmas season. They set the pace and provide the emotional tone. Their needs, which in our youth-oriented culture often shape family life, seem to be accorded even more importance during the holidays. The talk of Santa Claus, the emphasis on getting more and better toys, the intensified child-centered advertising campaigns, the last-minute preparations to make the gift-opening surprising and exciting — all of this effort on behalf of the children is the familiar routine for many families.

Some of the deepest satisfactions and most vivid memories of Christmas come when all this preparation reaches its climax and wide-eyed children spot their presents, open them with excitement and begin spontaneously to sort out their favorites. Somehow the animated faces of the youngsters makes all the fatiguing preparation seem worthwhile. These precious slices of family life should be treasured as privileged moments when the Gracious Mystery breaks through the ordinariness of life and reveals something of its hidden beauty and goodness. The clicking cameras on Christmas no doubt are often recording genuine religious experiences.

Valuable lessons and vital truths can be learned in our efforts to create a happy Christmas season for the children. The holidays are a great school for learning patience as the enthusiasm of the youngsters often creates trying situations. Encountering children's excessive material expectations can also teach us that the most valuable gifts involve the giving of self, doing things together, teaching restraint, allowing them to make mistakes and enabling them to do for themselves. Finally, trying to make children happy at Christmas reminds us of the essential gospel truth that we find ourselves by giving, that love liberates while selfishness constricts, that life feels richer when we can forget our own needs.

The experiences and insights gained from our child-oriented celebration of Christmas are valuable resources for shaping an authentic religious consciousness. But this approach is not sufficient in itself. This is obviously true for those who celebrate Christmas without youngsters around, but it also applies to parents who are immersed in the lives of their children.

Some of the disquiet, the vague dissatisfaction and even

Concrete Experiences

the depression which many people experience during the holiday season may be related to this total absorption in the life of children—especially if it precludes an adult celebration of Christmas. In this case genuine human needs are not met and the full meaning of the Incarnation is hidden.

Improving our celebration of Christmas, therefore, is not just a matter of fighting materialism, or remembering it is Christ's birthday, or teaching the youngsters Jesus' message to love others. Rather, we must respond better to the intrinsic power of the Incarnation to illumine and transform us in our quest for greater Christian maturity.

How might we move toward a more adult celebration of Christmas?

1) *Parents should give more conscious thought to their own spiritual growth during Advent.* What is gained if parents knock themselves out trying to make Christmas good for the kids and in the process become fatigued, on edge and impatient?

Christmas speaks of peace, but harried parents may find family life even less harmonious than usual. Perhaps parents would act more constructively if they followed an Advent program of regular spiritual reading, meditation and private prayer even if it meant fewer things done for the children.

Conscientious parents will benefit from taking time out for themselves by, for example, getting away from the house, recreating regularly, cultivating their own relationship and interacting with other adults. I know some effective parents who do this even if it takes some time away from the youngsters.

My own impression as a friendly observer is that many good parents are caught in the trap of trying to do too much for their children. As a result the youngsters develop unrealistic expectations of what life has to offer. Christmas simply heightens this tendency. Parents who fight this temptation and concentrate on achieving a deepened spiritual life during Advent will no doubt give a more valuable gift to their children on Christmas—one that will bear fruit throughout the year.

2) *As adults we should deepen our understanding of the Incarnation which constitutes the essential meaning of Christmas.*

The Incarnation is the good news that the mystery which encompasses our lives is not malicious or remote but benign and close. Our God draws near in the person of Jesus of Nazareth,

124

pitches his tent in our midst and guarantees the enduring
character of his love for us. We are not alone in this incredibly
vast universe but exist in partnership with a God who calls upon
us to build the world into a community of love. Our daily
struggle, our joys and our tears, are all transformed and given a
deeper meaning because they have been shared by the God-man.
Our bodies and this whole physical universe take on an added
dignity since God has forever joined himself to human nature in
the person of Jesus.

The story featuring a pregnant woman, a confused fiance,
a tiresome journey, a birth in a manager and a mysterious star
provides us with a concrete, earthy portrayal of the Good News
that God gives himself personally to us, making life in all its
ambiguity absolutely trustworthy. If the celebration of Christmas
actually gives us a deeper appreciation of this truth, we will not
find the joy of the season so fleeting.

3) *We must be transformed by the truth of the feast.* A
satisfying adult celebration of Christmas would require that a
genuine conversion of heart take place so that our actions are
more in tune with the deepest meaning of God living personally
in our midst.

We can get hold of an important aspect of this meaning
by recalling that Christmas is the birth of the Prince of Peace.
Jesus came to free people, to form a community of love for all,
to minister to the alienated, to challenge the abuse of power and
to oppose violence. If we allowed this message of peace to
transform our hearts, we would become more effective
peacemakers in our families, neighborhoods and parishes. If we
put on the mind of the Prince of Peace we might find ourselves
working more actively for disarmament, for a reasonable defense
budget and for harmony among nations. By responding in this
constructive way we would carry the true meaning of the
Christmas season throughout the year.

An adult celebration of the definitive and permanent
joining of God and the human race demands more than verbal
assent and a brief period of rejoicing. Good news of such
magnitude and significance calls for a conversion of heart and a
continuing effort to live out its implications in the real world.

Many of us carry with us happy childhood memories and
warm images of Christmas: going to church, trimming the tree,

exchanging gifts, sharing a special meal and feeling loved. It is important that we provide such happy memories for the next generation while keeping before them the true meaning of the feast.

We have also come to know the disappointments connected with the holidays—ideals tarnished, joy lost, expectations unrealized, peace delayed. In response, it will do us little good to attempt a nostalgic return to childhood days. Instead, we need to find our own ways of moving toward a more mature celebration of Christmas.

If we make a genuine effort to achieve spiritual growth, to deepen our understanding of the Incarnation and to respond to its authentic meaning, we may find surprising nourishment for our empty hearts. The smiles of happy youngsters bring us joy; a proper celebration of Christmas reveals the deepest source and continuing power of that joy.

Thanksgiving: Integrating Religion and Culture

The celebration of Thanksgiving in the United States is an intriguing mix of religion and culture, piety and patriotism. Our imaginations have been touched by Thanksgiving meals as well as Eucharistic celebrations, by turkey and pumpkin pie as well as bread and wine, by Uncle Sam as well as Jesus Christ. We gather on Thanksgiving as both believers and citizens, and we thank God for both religious liberty and political freedom.

Of course the interaction between faith and patriotism highlighted on Thanksgiving is part of an ongoing relationship. We are always Church members and citizens; our allegiance is expressed to the cross and the flag. We live in the City of God and the City of Man; our time is spent with parish and community. It is important for us to make sense out of this mix, to understand how faith and patriotism influence our minds and hearts and to establish a proper relationship between them.

How do cross and flag interact in my own life? Various responses to the question are possible.

At one extreme some will baptize the culture and accept it uncritically. "My country right or wrong" becomes the slogan; "Love it or leave it" is the practical advice. There is no tension between being a believer and a citizen. The flag has become judge of the cross, obscuring the prophetic power of the gospel.

At the other extreme some Christians take a totally negative attitude toward our American culture, either remaining totally indifferent toward it or actively fighting against it. The world belongs to the devil and is totally untouched by the Spirit. Grace is in the Church and not in the culture. When the cross judges the flag, the flag is found to be without merit or value.

In searching for a middle ground between these two extremes, we can start with these theological premises: that the Father loves the world, that Christ has redeemed all people, that the Spirit is at work in all human existence, that grace can penetrate the social order, and that the whole of creation groans until it shares in the final victory. At the same time, it is evident that sin continues to contend with the more powerful grace at work in the world. Thus, one expects aspects of truth and goodness to emerge from human culture while realizing that deception and evil are also present.

In this theology, the high point of the process in which God communicates himself to the world is found in Jesus of Nazareth. Thus Christ, as witnessed in the Scripture and proclaimed in the Church, is for us the norm by which we judge the culture.

The cross, therefore, is clearly judge of the flag, but it expects to find a measure of goodness and truth in the reality represented by the flag. The believer possesses a wisdom and power which can not only criticize the culture, but which can transform it. With a growing realization that sin is embedded in institutions and systems, Christians today must join together with the Lord in struggling for social justice.

When we contemplate Thanksgiving from this theological perspective, we can find much of truth and value to be celebrated and encouraged. Historically, the celebration has been a genuine

127

response to the perception that we have been blessed by God. In 1621, after a severe winter and first harvest, William Bradford, governor of Plymouth Colony, inaugurated a three-day thanksgiving celebration which included the Indians who had helped the Pilgrims survive. It is, of course, this celebration, with its clear religious message of gratitude to the Supreme Being, which continues to impress itself on the imagination of each succeeding generation of citizens of the United States. When President Washington proclaimed a nationwide day of thanksgiving in 1789, he made it clear that the day should be devoted to prayer and expressions of gratitude to God.

The idea of setting aside a specific day for offering special thanks to God gradually spread throughout the states, aided in the middle part of the 19th century by the urging of Sarah Joseph Hale, editor of a widely read women's magazine. In 1863, when President Lincoln invited all citizens to observe the last Thursday of November as a national day of thanksgiving, it was in order to give "thanks and praise to our beneficent Father who dwelleth in the heavens."

Over the years many secular features were added to the Thanksgiving celebration: parades sponsored by department stores such as Gimbel's in Philadelphia and Macy's in New York and football games beginning with the Yale-Princeton game in 1876. And in 1941, when Thanksgiving finally became a legal holiday to be celebrated on the fourth Thursday of November, much of the background debate had to do with economic considerations, especially the desire of business people to keep the holiday as far away from Christmas as possible. Despite these secular and materialistic factors, the real meaning of Thanksgiving, represented by the annual proclamations of presidents and governors, has always been to recognize the great blessings bestowed on our nation by Divine Providence.

Our Thanksgiving celebrations today continue to manifest a great deal of genuine religious sentiment reflecting authentic Christian values. Extended families gather together, often at considerable personal sacrifice. Individuals sense that this should be a time of harmony, peace and reconciliation. The traditional meal becomes a ritual in which family stories are recalled, shared values are celebrated and hopes for the future are surfaced. Many people respond generously at this time to the plight of the poor who need food, clothing and opportunities to help themselves.

The contrast between the noise, busyness and hype surrounding Christmas and the simpler celebration of Thanksgiving is striking and instructive. Most people find themselves struggling to maintain some measure of inner peace during the harried month of December. The significance of the celebration of the coming of the Lord is often lost in the midst of consumerism and gift-giving. In contrast, the celebration of Thanksgiving moves at a slower pace allowing for reflection on blessings received and values treasured. Spared the stress of mandatory gift-giving, we can concentrate on the personal relationships which bring our deepest joys. The traditional intent of Thanksgiving to express gratitude to Divine Providence for our blessings continues to shape our celebration despite all the efforts to secularize our national holiday.

As Christians we can wholeheartedly affirm the spirit of gratitude, reconciliation and generosity which surrounds Thanksgiving. For us Divine Providence takes on a clearer countenance in the person of Jesus Christ who taught us to call God our Father. Our Eucharistic meals reveal to us the deepest meaning of our Thanksgiving dinner. As we reflect on our national holiday from this perspective, we can rejoice in the inner harmony we experience as Christians and as citizens of the United States.

In addition to affirming the positive values and meanings represented by Thanksgiving, the gospel moves us to examine our culture for inconsistencies, failed ideals, societal contradictions and anti-Christian tendencies. Being a Christian in the United States can raise difficult questions. Serious believers know tension and dissonance as well as peace and harmony. I recall a man who worked in a welfare agency telling me that Thanksgiving was a traumatic holiday for him. He felt a deep disquiet as he reflected on his own material abundance in contrast to the poverty endured by the people he served.

Honest reflection on Thanksgiving cannot ignore this gap between those who roam freely through the affluent society and those caught in the hellish circle of poverty. The gospel forces attention on the needy who live on the margins and miss the safety nets. From the perspective of Jesus Christ the liberator, the powerless come into view as brothers and sisters who deserve a chance to take charge of their own destiny. The contemporary Christian cannot ignore the societal contradictions and the structural injustices which enslave fellow citizens in this land of abundance.

The statistics are grim enough, with over 33 million people living below the poverty line. But the real impact comes when we look into the eyes of a malnourished child, hear the frustration in the voice of an unemployed man, feel the fatigue of the mother struggling to feed her three children on food stamps, and sense the anxiety of the elderly woman trying to survive on a fixed income. All of this within a nation of unprecedented wealth.

If we allow the gospel to turn our eyes outward, we see poverty beyond anything known here: Innocent children dying of starvation, masses of people struggling to survive one more day, whole nations suffering because of the greed of the privileged. And again the real shock comes when individual faces of the oppressed and suffering appear on our television screens, almost as if struggling to break through our jaded consciousness. All of this suffering occurs while we as a nation enjoy an affluence beyond the dreams of most people in the world. The often-quoted statistic is familiar but telling: We who live in the United States constitute about six percent of the world's population, and yet we consume about 40 percent of the world's resources. It is possible to think that we are God's chosen people and deserve such abundance, or that our innate goodness as a nation calls forth the Lord's blessings on us, or that our capitalistic system is so productive because it is God's very own economic system. It is not hard to find this "chosen people" viewpoint even among those who give their allegiance to Jesus of Nazareth.

Our meditation on the deeper meaning of Thanksgiving challenges these assumptions and suggests positive action. As followers of Jesus, who came to liberate captives and set the downtrodden free, we must be attentive to the cries of the poor and oppressed in our world today. The gospel calls us to overcome the arrogance lurking in the "chosen people" notion by recognizing all people as members of God's family. Our Catholic social teaching insists that rich nations such as ours should come to the aid of underdeveloped countries so that all nations can live in peaceful interdependence. Christians today who are becoming more aware of social sin and systemic evil must band together to transform these unjust structures.

As we reflect honestly on the meaning of Thanksgiving we cannot neglect the plight of the poor, whether at home or abroad. When the cross judges the flag, contradictions and failed ideals are painfully clear. We who enjoy abundance are called not only to speak words of gratitude but also to take constructive action to help liberate poor and needy people.

Autumn: Letting Go of Summer Dreams

"I hate fall," she said with a hint of both sadness and frustration in her voice. Autumn always brought, as far back as she could remember, a mysterious sense of despondency, a vague uneasiness which could easily slide into depression. In our counseling session I did not investigate the meaning or roots of this statement but concentrated on positive responses to her generally unhappy situation.

During my usual post-encounter reflection, I realized that the real depth of her problem had eluded me. Perhaps I was not tuned in because for me the fall has so many positive resonances. The distinctive beauty of the season is a good catalyst for my prayers and reflections. As the color emerges in the changing leaves, deeper levels of my being are touched: longings which are beyond words; a sense of homelessness which can only hope for a final resting place; a bittersweet anticipation of a love which seems always disappointing, but mysteriously holds promise of fulfillment. Expressed more concretely, I find that prayer comes naturally when I drive slowly along a road lined with the rich reds and golds of the changing leaves.

A large part of fall's fascination for me has to do with the world of athletics. Memories and images flood my mind: Exciting pennant races which go down to the final few games of the season. A leisurely stroll across a leaf-strewn campus to the football stadium for an exciting game played in beautiful weather. Beginning practice for the start of the basketball season. Playing a last round of golf during Indian summer. And, most of all, the World Series. It symbolizes the fruit of sustained effort over the long haul as well as the joy of participating even if victory is denied.

Fall resonates with a dominant mood of my psyche. Autumn's melancholic language is as familar as my very breathing. True, the brilliant leaves will soon be gone and Indian summer's glory is filled with the approach of winter. Even the World Series produces champions who become also-rans. Still the resonating feels good. It is affirming of my deepest instincts. Since melancholy is acceptable in the fall, I can, for a time, feel in tune with the very rhythms of nature during this season.

When I return to the problem of understanding the woman's negative feelings about autumn, my intuition says it has little to do with fall and a great deal to do with leaving summer behind. Of course the approach of winter, which represents death itself, could also be the problem; but in this case, I doubt it. I am inclined to put the emphasis on the passing of summer, which symbolizes freedom, leisure, lack of constraint, travel and opportunities for self-expression. Summer carries expectations along these lines even if they are not realized. The season of sun and warmth recalls a time of innocence, of childlike trust, of dreams with no limits. Summer begins with the joyful expectations of Memorial Day and ends with the sadness of Labor Day. It is as though someone has officially declared that the time of innocence is over—no more free-floating, spontaneous fun. The time of joy, leisure and levity has ended. Now you must enter the real world which is organized around the numbered motion of the clock and is dominated by authority figures who demand hard work and the repression of instinct.

The movement from summer to fall annually reenacts our transition from childhood to adulthood. For some people this is a painful reminder that innocence lost cannot be regained. In the real world we cannot romp around in a totally carefree manner. We are condemned to care and that can be painful.

Perhaps the woman is upset because the summer was disappointing. It went too fast; the vacation was boring; and catch-up tasks were left undone. But this does not compute. It is more likely that she is dealing with repressed rage over the loss of what summer essentially signifies—a time of playful innocence when the world can be trusted and one's instincts can be followed.

Fall symbolizes the intrusion of harsh reality into a life of simple fun and spontaneous pleasure. "I hate fall" means "I protest against this horrible invasion into my lighthearted world." It is like lying down on the floor and kicking one's feet in sheer rage against the unfairness of this turn of events: "How dare anyone or anything violate the childlike coziness of my existence!" Fall carries negative significance if it symbolizes the destruction of the utopian dream of childhood that life can be happy without end.

If this is a correct analysis, then "I hate fall" has emanated from the very core of this woman's being, representing a massive protest against the essential unfairness of life itself.

Even those of us who love the fall can recognize the problem when put in these terms. How are we to cope with being expelled from the Garden of Eden? How do we deal with a world which challenges our expectations of order and fairness? What protests against reality lurk in our own heart, and how do we respond to them? Are we in touch with our yearning for paradise, and how do we handle the frustration of living in an imperfect world? When we confront monstrous evil, how do we control our rage and maintain our hope?

There are, of course, no simple or adequate answers to the problems raised by the loss of innocence. We do have, however, two fundamental options once we discover that our idyllic dreams cannot survive in the real world.

The first alternative is to live with deep rage and total protest against this attack on our longings for control and order. Persons choosing this option can either rail against the unfairness of it all and live with cynical pessimism, or they can try to repress the rage which leads to periodic outbursts of inappropriate anger. Such rage can slant a person's perception so that all the tiny hurts and frustrations of life are seen as proofs of the essential unfairness of it all.

The second alternative is to strive to accept reality on its own terms. This means living in the real world using escapes sparingly and insightfully. It involves recognizing that all human beings must contend with the evil and suffering built into human existence.

Self-acceptance is at the center of this option. We must recognize both our strengths and weaknesses as well as our potential and limitations. The key is to recognize and accept our absolute and total dependency on the trustworthy One who will one day fulfill all our dreams.

If I get another chance to talk to this woman, I will tell her stories of other individuals who were able to let go of their deep rage over the unfairness of life. They quit protecting themselves from reality and opened themselves to the Divine Spirit. They learned that a process which shatters carefree dreams can still be trusted because it is guided and supported by the Gracious Mystery which eventually brings us back to Paradise.

Epilogue
A Contemporary Creed

After looking at isolated bits of human experience in the various reflections in this book, it is helpful to come back to an organic understanding of the Christian faith. Short creeds help us to do that. The following contemporary summary of the Christian faith is an effort to express an integrated understanding of our beliefs.

We human beings experience ourselves as essentially mysterious. For example, we long for a love both satisfying and imperishable. When we experience intimations of this kind of love, we rejoice, sensing that it is coming from a source beyond our control. And when we are inevitably frustrated in this quest by our own limitations as well as those of the beloved, we are moved to ask whether this desire is doomed to eternal frustration or whether it will find an ultimate fulfillment in a goal beyond our imagining.

Another mysterious aspect of our experience is the troubling battle we know within ourselves between constructive and destructive tendencies. *Angels and demons fight for control of our soul.*

This raises the question of the relative power of good and evil in ourselves and our world. There is no denying that we are threatened by sin and that evil is embedded in our societal systems. These harsh facts are reflected in our doctrine of "original sin." Our faith-inspired position, however, is: *The forces of good are more powerful than all the evil*; a healing, transforming power is at work in our world; the work of creation, ourselves included, possesses an essential goodness.

The good news is that we are loved despite our unworthiness and that we are accepted despite our limitations.

In our knowing, loving and struggling, *we can recognize ourselves as related to a source and goal which always exceeds our grasp.* It seems appropriate to refer to this essentially incomprehensible and inexhaustible power as "the Mystery." The core of our belief system insists that this mystery is on our side, can be trusted and addresses us personally. Therefore we describe it as the gracious Mystery and call it "God." This deity is not a particular being or one aspect of our total experience but the personal condition, backdrop, horizon, basis, ground and fulfillment of everything we are and do.

The Mystery both fascinates and strikes us as awesome. *We experience ourselves at times as hovering over a dark abyss but we believe that if we let go we will fall into gracious hands.* It is the Mystery which allures us into the unknown future and promises us a final fulfillment of all our deepest longings. We call this "salvation" and believe we already have a partial share in this blessing as we journey toward our final goal.

We believe that the Mystery does not remain aloof from our concerns or merely send us messages from afar. Rather, *the Gracious One enters into our history, penetrates our experience, surrounds our existence, knocks at our hearts and calls to our spirit.* This personal self-giving which we call "grace" modifies our existence, changes our consciousness and echoes in our mind and heart. It creates a universal revelation which has been experienced by all human beings through the call of conscience, the intuition of truth, the attraction of goodness and the allure of beauty.

When individuals respond positively to this revelation, they enter into a transforming relationship with the Mystery which we call "justifying grace." *The "yes" to the call of conscience and the search for truth constitutes a saving faith and makes us dwelling places of the Spirit.*

The extent and intensity of the communication of the Mystery depends on the receptivity of the individual. Those who have been blessed with greater openness along with the ability to interpret this relationship correctly are called "prophets." We do not hesitate to give this title to the Buddha and Mohammed as well as Moses and Isaiah.

But our hearts yearn for a final prophet, for one with the definitive word from the deity, for an individual worthy of absolute trust, for one who carries all the hopes of humankind, for the savior who conquers even death. The good news is that such a one has appeared in our history. We know him as a carpenter from Nazareth, an itinerant teacher, master storyteller, proclaimer of the kingdom, friend of outcasts, example of love, miracle worker, shaker of the establishment, innocent victim, crucified Lord and resurrected Savior.

Jesus of Nazareth surpasses all previous prophets and will be superseded by none in the future. Here is a man, like us in all things but sin, who is so open, so responsive, so obedient to the Mystery (which he addressed in the most familiar fashion as *Abba*) that it is true to say that *he is God personally present to us.* In our history, therefore, God's self-giving and human receptivity have reached a never-to-be-surpassed high point in Jesus of Nazareth. We call this union the "Incarnation" and view Jesus not merely as a great ethical teacher but as cosmic Lord and son of God.

It was in his death that Jesus definitively completed a lifetime of dedication to doing the will of Abba. With his cause going badly, his friends deserting him, his message of peace misunderstood, Jesus surrendered himself totally and finally to his Father. And in this very act of self-sacrificing love his cause was won, his teaching vindicated, his obedience rewarded, his life renewed, his spirit shared. We call this action of God on behalf of Jesus the "resurrection" and see it as the center point of our faith.

We desperately want to believe that the good will triumph, that love will prove stronger than death, that our efforts will be rewarded, that we will live a richer life forever. The resurrection of Jesus tells us that we can indeed believe this to be true. The continuing struggle from Adam onward between grace and sin is now irrevocably decided in favor of grace. History will reach its appointed goal, the flow of life is toward salvation, the final victory of good and truth is assured.

Those of us who believe Christ is the absolute savior sense the need for support and challenge and so we join together

in a community. We call this community "the Church." Our
desire for rootedness is partially satisfied by remaining in
solidarity with the early followers of Jesus who preserved their
witness to him in the sacred writings we call the "New
Testament." These writings still provide the guiding norm for our
own faith in Christ.

Since Jesus no longer walks the earth in visible fashion,
we need a reminder of his continuing presence. We strive to be
such a sign in our local communities or parishes where the Word
is preached, the Lord's Supper is celebrated, the needy are served
and evil is challenged. It is our great responsibility as a
community to become a better sign of the Lord's presence; and
it is our great sadness that our divisions, selfishness, prejudice
and inequities diminish the power of our witness.

*The members of our community take seriously the Lord's
essential call to love our neighbor and our God.* We experience,
however, a continuing and painful gap between our ideals and
our performance. We know the truth of the statement, "I am a
Christian in order to become one." Parts of our personality seem
to be out of tune with our fundamental decision to follow the
Lord. We are prepared to admit our free, culpable failures to
grow in love. We believe, however, that the God who calls us
by name always forgives those sins and thereby empowers us to
move toward greater integration and a more encompassing
charity.

*While we believe that the Gracious Mystery is at work in
the whole world strengthening and healing, it is in accord with
our bodily nature to symbolize and make visible this presence in
sacred signs.* We call these sacred signs "sacraments." Through
these special signs the Church makes itself visible and operative.
And at key moments of need in our life cycle we encounter the
risen Lord through these sacred celebrations. In the greatest of
these signs, the sacred meal called the "Eucharist" or "Lord's
Supper," we recall God's goodness to us and offer our worship
to the Father in union with the risen Lord.

The journey which constitutes our common life moves
inexorably toward death. From the perspective of faith *we can
see death as our freest act* in which we are called upon to imitate
the Lord in surrendering completely to the Gracious Mystery. In
doing so we believe that we break through a barrier into a richer,

fuller life of love in union with Christ and those who have preceded us.

Finally, *we envision the ultimate consummation of the work of Christ*: The new heaven and new earth are established; the whole of creation and history reaches its fulfillment; the entire human family is joined in solidarity; and *the Gracious Mystery is all in all.*

Also by Jim Bacik...

Thoughtful, challenging talks on cassette from St. Anthony Messenger Press:

The Process of Conversion: *A Self-Examination for Growing in the Christian Life*. Set of two tapes in vinyl binder: CAS 390 $18.95

Knowing Jesus Christ. Boxed set of two 90-minute cassettes: CAS 340 $16.95

Understanding the Faith: *In Search of a Contemporary Theology*. Boxed set of seven 90-minute cassettes: CAS 220 $62.95

To order any of these cassette series, or for information on all St. Anthony Messenger Press books, tapes and periodicals, write to St. Anthony Messenger Press, 1615 Republic St., Cincinnati, OH 45210, or call 513-241-5615.